INHIBITIONS, SYMPTOMS
AND ANXIETY

By SIGMUND FREUD

THE STANDARD EDITION

OF THE COMPLETE PSYCHOLOGICAL WORKS OF

SIGMUND FREUD

24 VOLUMES

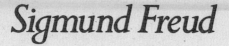

Sigmund Freud

INHIBITIONS, SYMPTOMS AND ANXIETY

TRANSLATED BY
Alix Strachey

REVISED AND EDITED BY
James Strachey

WITH A BIOGRAPHICAL
INTRODUCTION BY
Peter Gay

W·W·NORTON & COMPANY
New York · London

Library of Congress Cataloging in Publication Data
Freud, Sigmund, 1856-1939.
  Inhibitions, symptoms and anxiety.
  Translation of Hemmung, Symptom und Angst.
  Bibliography: p.
  Includes index.
  1. Anxiety. 2. Neuroses. 3. Psychoanalysis. I. Title.
RC531.F7413 1977 616.8'52 77-22051

ISBN 0-393-00874-6

W. W. Norton & Company, Inc. is also the publisher of The Standard
Edition of the Complete Psychological Works of Sigmund Freud.

W. W. Norton & Company, Inc.
500 Fifth Avenue New York, N.Y. 10110
W. W. Norton & Company Ltd.
37 Great Russell Street London WC1B 3NU

PRINTED IN THE UNITED STATES OF AMERICA
1 2 3 4 5 6 7 8 9 0

Contents

SIGMUND FREUD: A BRIEF LIFE

by Peter Gay

It was Freud's fate, as he observed not without pride, to "agitate the sleep of mankind." Half a century after his death, it seems clear that he succeeded far better than he expected, though in ways he would not have appreciated. It is commonplace but true that we all speak Freud now, correctly or not. We casually refer to oedipal conflicts and sibling rivalry, narcissism and Freudian slips. But before we can speak that way with authority, we must read his writings attentively. They repay reading, with dividends.

Sigmund Freud was born on May 6, 1856, in the small Moravian town of Freiberg.[1] His father, Jacob Freud, was an impecunious merchant; his mother, Amalia, was handsome, self-assertive, and young—twenty years her husband's junior and his third wife. Jacob Freud had two sons from his first marriage who were about Amalia Freud's age and lived nearby. One of these half brothers had a son, John, who, though Sigmund Freud's nephew, was older than his uncle.

[1]His given names were Sigismund Schlomo, but he never used his middle name and, after experimenting with the shorter form for some time, definitively adopted the first name Sigmund—on occasion relapsing into the original formulation—in the early 1870s, when he was a medical student at the University of Vienna. Freiberg, now in Czechoslovakia, bears the Czech name "Pribor."

Freud's family constellation, then, was intricate enough to puzzle the clever and inquisitive youngster. Inquisitiveness, the natural endowment of children, was particularly marked in him. Life would provide ample opportunity to satisfy it.

In 1860, when Freud was almost four, he moved with his family to Vienna, then a magnet for many immigrants. This was the opening phase of the Hapsburg Empire's liberal era. Jews, only recently freed from onerous taxes and humiliating restrictions on their property rights, professional choices, and religious practices, could realistically harbor hopes for economic advancement, political participation, and a measure of social acceptance. This was the time, Freud recalled, when "every industrious Jewish school boy carried a Cabinet Minister's portfolio in his satchel."[2] The young Freud was encouraged to cultivate high ambitions. As his mother's first-born and a family favorite, he secured, once his family could afford it, a room of his own. He showed marked gifts from his first school days, and in his secondary school, or Gymnasium, he was first in his class year after year.

In 1873, at seventeen, Freud entered the University of Vienna. He had planned to study law, but, driven on by what he called his "greed for knowledge," instead matriculated in the faculty of medicine, intending to embark, not on a conventional career as a physician, but on philosophical-scientific investigations that might solve some of the great riddles that fascinated him. He found his work in physiology and neurology so absorbing that he did not take his degree until 1881.

A brilliant researcher, he cultivated the habit of close observation and the congenial stance of scientific skepticism. He was privileged to work under professors with international reputations, almost all German imports and tough-

---

[2] *The Interpretation of Dreams* (1900), *SE* IV, 193.

minded positivists who disdained metaphysical speculations about, let alone pious explanations of, natural phenomena. Even after Freud modified their theories of the mind—in essence barely disguised physiological theories—he recalled his teachers with unfeigned gratitude. The most memorable of them, Ernst Brücke, an illustrious physiologist and a civilized but exacting taskmaster, confirmed Freud's bent as an unbeliever. Freud had grown up with no religious instruction at home, came to Vienna University as an atheist, and left it as an atheist—with persuasive scientific arguments.

In 1882, on Brücke's advice, Freud reluctantly left the laboratory to take a lowly post at the Vienna General Hospital. The reason was romantic: in April, he had met Martha Bernays, a slender, attractive young woman from northern Germany visiting one of his sisters, and fallen passionately in love. He was soon secretly engaged to her, but too poor to establish the respectable bourgeois household that he and his fiancée thought essential. It was not until September 1886, some five months after opening his practice in Vienna, with the aid of wedding gifts and loans from affluent friends, that the couple could marry. Within nine years, they had six children, the last of whom, Anna, grew up to be her father's confidante, secretary, nurse, disciple, and representative, and an eminent psychoanalyst in her own right.

Before his marriage, from October 1885 to February 1886, Freud worked in Paris with the celebrated French neurologist Jean-Martin Charcot, who impressed Freud with his bold advocacy of hypnosis as an instrument for healing medical disorders, and no less bold championship of the thesis (then quite unfashionable) that hysteria is an ailment to which men are susceptible no less than women. Charcot, an unrivaled observer, stimulated Freud's growing interest in the theoretical and therapeutic aspects of mental healing. Nervous ailments became Freud's specialty, and in the 1890s, as he told a friend, psychology became his tyrant. During these years he founded the psychoanalytic theory of mind.

He had intriguing if somewhat peculiar help. In 1887, he had met a nose-and-throat specialist from Berlin, Wilhelm Fliess, and rapidly established an intimate friendship with him. Fliess was the listener the lonely Freud craved: an intellectual gambler shocked at no idea, a propagator of provocative (at times fruitful) theories, an enthusiast who fed Freud ideas on which he could build. For over a decade, Fliess and Freud exchanged confidential letters and technical memoranda, meeting occasionally to explore their subversive notions. And Freud was propelled toward the discovery of psychoanalysis in his practice: his patients proved excellent teachers. He was increasingly specializing in women suffering from hysteria, and, observing their symptoms and listening to their complaints, he found that, though a good listener, he did not listen carefully enough. They had much to tell him.

In 1895, Freud and his fatherly friend Josef Breuer, a thriving, generous internist, published *Studies on Hysteria,* assigning Breuer's former patient "Anna O." pride of place. She had furnished fascinating material for intimate conversations between Breuer and Freud, and was to become, quite against her—and Breuer's—will, the founding patient of psychoanalysis. She demonstrated to Freud's satisfaction that hysteria originates in sexual malfunctioning and that symptoms can be talked away.

The year 1895 was decisive for Freud in other ways. In July, Freud managed to analyze a dream, his own, fully. He would employ this dream, known as "Irma's injection," as a model for psychoanalytic dream interpretation when he published it, some four years later, in his *Interpretation of*

Dreams. In the fall, he drafted, but neither completed nor published, what was later called the Project for a Scientific Psychology. It anticipated some of his fundamental theories yet serves as a reminder that Freud had been deeply enmeshed in the traditional physiological interpretation of mental events.

Increasingly Freud was offering psychological explanations for psychological phenomena. In the spring of 1896, he first used the fateful name, "psychoanalysis." Then in October his father died; "the most important event," he recalled a dozen years later, "the most poignant loss, of a man's life."[3] It supplied a powerful impetus toward psychoanalytic theorizing, stirring Freud to his unprecedented self-analysis, more systematic and thoroughgoing than the frankest autobiographer's self-probing. In the next three or four years, as he labored over his "Dream book," new discoveries crowded his days. But first he had to jettison the "seduction theory" he had championed for some time. It held that *every* neurosis results from premature sexual activity, mainly child molestation, in childhood.[4] Once freed from this far-reaching but improbable theory, Freud could appreciate the share of fantasies in mental life, and discover the Oedipus complex, that universal family triangle.

Freud's *Interpretation of Dreams* was published in November 1899.[5] It treated all dreams as wish fulfillments, detailed the mental stratagems that translate their causes into the strange drama the awakening dreamer remembers,

---

[3]Ibid., xxvi.

[4]Freud never claimed that sexual abuse does not exist. He had patients who he knew had not imagined the assaults they reported. All he abandoned when he abandoned the seduction theory was the sweeping claim that *only* the rape of a child, whether a boy or a girl, by a servant, an older sibling, or a classmate, could be the cause of a neurosis.

[5]The book bears the date of 1900 on the title page and this date is usually given as the date of publication.

and, in the difficult seventh chapter, outlined a comprehensive theory of mind. Its first reception was cool. During six years, only 351 copies were sold; a second edition did not appear until 1909. However, Freud's popularly written *Psychopathology of Everyday Life* of 1901 found a wider audience. Its collection of appealing slips of all sorts made Freud's fundamental point that the mind, however disheveled it might appear, is governed by firm rules. Thus—to give but one typical instance—the presiding officer of the Austrian parliament, facing a disagreeable season, opened it with the formal declaration that it was hereby closed. That "accident" had been prompted by his hidden repugnance for the sessions ahead.

Gradually, though still considered a radical, Freud acquired prestige and supporters. He had quarreled with Fliess in 1900, and, though their correspondence lingered on for some time, the two men never met again. Yet in 1902, after unconscionable delays, apparently generated by anti-Semitism combined with distrust of the maverick innovator, he was finally appointed an associate professor at the University of Vienna. Late that year, Freud and four other Viennese physicians began meeting every Wednesday night in his apartment at Berggasse 19 to discuss psychoanalytic questions; four years after, the group, grown to over a dozen regular participants, employed a paid secretary (Otto Rank) to take minutes and keep records. Finally, in 1908, it was transformed into the Vienna Psychoanalytic Society. At least some medical men (and a few women) were taking Freud's ideas seriously.

In 1905, Freud buttressed the structure of psychoanalytic thought with the second pillar of his theory: the *Three Essays on the Theory of Sexuality.* It outlined perversions and "normal" development from childhood to puberty with a lack of censoriousness and an openness hitherto virtually unknown in medical literature. Again in 1905, Freud brought out his book on jokes and the first of his famous case histories: "Fragment of an Analysis of a Case of Hysteria," nicknamed the "Dora case." He published it to illustrate the uses of dream interpretation in psychoanalysis, and expose his failure to recognize the power of transference in the analytic situation, but its lack of empathy with his embattled teen-age analysand has made it controversial.

In the following decade, Freud enriched the technique of psychoanalysis with three more sophisticated case histories—"Analysis of a Phobia in a Five-Year-Old Boy" ("Little Hans"), "Notes upon a Case of Obsessional Neurosis" ("Rat Man") in 1909, and "Psycho-Analytic Notes on an Autobiographical Account of a Case of Paranoia" ("Schreber Case") in 1911. Despite recent reanalyses, they remain lucid expository models across a wide spectrum of mental ailments. Then, from 1910 on, Freud published pioneering, exceedingly influential papers on technique, to establish psychoanalytic method on sound foundations. Nor did he neglect theory; witness such an important paper as "Formulations on the Two Principles of Mental Functioning" (1911), in which he differentiated between the "primary process," the primitive, unconscious element in the mind, and the "secondary process," largely conscious and controlled.

During these years, Freud also broke out of the circumscribed bounds of clinical and theoretical specialization by publishing papers on religion, literature, sexual mores, biography, sculpture, prehistory, and much else. "Obsessive Actions and Religious Practices" (1907), "Creative Writers and Daydreaming" (1908), " 'Civilized' Sexual Morality and Modern Nervous Illness" (1908), and his widely debated study of the origins of homosexuality, "Leonardo da Vinci and a Memory of His Childhood" (1910), are only samples of his range. Freud took all of culture as his province. He was realizing the program he had outlined for himself in his youth: to solve some of the great riddles of human existence.

Yet Freud also found the decade from 1905 to 1914 agitating with the progress of, and disagreeable splits within, a rapidly emerging international movement—*his* movement. Psychoanalytic politics took center stage. Two principal sources of hope for the future of Freud's ideas, and later of envenomed contention, were the intelligent, Socialist Viennese physician Alfred Adler (1870–1937), and the original, self-willed Swiss psychiatrist Carl G. Jung (1875–1961). Adler had been among Freud's earliest adherents and remained for some years his most prominent Viennese advocate. But as professional interest in psychoanalysis—not all of it benevolent—grew apace, as Freud's upsetting ideas were being explored at psychiatrists' congresses, Freud aspired to enlarge the reach of psychoanalysis beyond its place of origin. Vienna, with its handful of followers, struck him as provincial, unsuitable as headquarters.

The first breakthrough came in 1906, when Jung, then principal psychiatrist at the renowned clinic Burghölzli in Zurich, sent Freud an offprint. Freud responded promptly; a cordial correspondence blossomed, and the friendship was cemented by Jung's visit to Freud in early 1907. Freud was only fifty, vigorous and productive, but he had long brooded on himself as aging and decrepit. He was seeking a successor who would carry the psychoanalytic dispensation to later generations and into a world larger than the Viennese, Jewish ambiance to which psychoanalysis was then confined. Jung, a formidable presence and energetic debater, was an inspired discovery: he was not old, he was not Viennese, he was not Jewish. Jung was prominent in the first international congress of psychoanalysts at Salzburg in the spring of 1908, and was appointed, the following year, editor of a newly founded *Yearbook.* Freud, delighted with Jung, anointed him his son, his crown prince—accolades that Jung welcomed, indeed encouraged. Hence, when the International Psychoanalytic Association was founded in March 1910, in Nürnberg, Jung was Freud's logical, inevitable, choice for president. Freud's Viennese adherents saw their city displaced by Zurich as the center of psychoanalysis, and did not like it. A compromise was hammered out, and for some time peace reigned in the Vienna Psychoanalytic Society. But Adler was developing distinctive psychological ideas, which featured aggressiveness over sexuality, and "organ inferiority" as a dominant cause of neuroses. A split became inevitable, and, in the summer of 1911, Adler and some of his adherents resigned, leaving Freud and the Freudians in control of the Vienna society.

Freud was not without accolades. In September 1909, he had received an honorary doctorate at Clark University in Worcester, Massachusetts, as had Jung. But like Adler, Jung increasingly diverged from Freud's ideas. He had never been easy with the prominence Freud assigned to the sexual drive—libido. By early 1912, these reservations took a personal turn. In response, Ernest Jones, Freud's principal English lieutenant, formed a defensive secret band of likeminded analysts, the Committee. It consisted of himself, Freud, Sandor Ferenczi (a brilliant adherent from Budapest), the witty Viennese lawyer Hanns Sachs, the astute Berlin clinician and theorist Karl Abraham, and Freud's amanuensis, the autodidact Otto Rank. It seemed needed: by late 1912, the correspondence between Jung and Freud had grown acrimonious and in January 1914, Freud terminated his friendship with Jung. A split was only a matter of time; in the spring of 1914, Jung resigned from his powerful positions in the psychoanalytic movement.

The strains of psychoanalytic politics did not keep Freud

from continuing his explorations of an impressive variety of topics. In 1913, he published an audacious, highly speculative venture into psychoanalytic prehistory, *Totem and Taboo*, which specified the moment that savages, in some dim, remote past, entered culture by murdering their father and acquiring guilt feelings. Then, in 1914, he published (anonymously) "The Moses of Michelangelo," uniting his admiration for Michelangelo's brooding sculpture with his powers of observation. In the same year, with an unsettling paper on narcissism, he subverted crucial aspects of psychoanalytic thought by throwing doubts upon his theory of drives—hitherto divided into erotic and egoistic.

But harrowing events on the world stage shouldered aside Freud's reassessment of psychoanalytic theory. On June 28, 1914, Austria's Archduke Francis Ferdinand and his consort were assassinated. Six weeks later, on August 4, Europe was at war. The first casualty for psychoanalysis was Freud's eventually best-known case history, "From the History of an Infantile Neurosis" ("Wolf Man"), written in the fall of 1914, but not published until 1918. Psychoanalytic activity almost ground to a halt. Many potential patients were at the front; most psychoanalysts were drafted into the medical corps; communications between "enemies" like Ernest Jones and Freud were severely truncated; psychoanalytic publications almost vanished; and congresses, the lifeblood of communication, were out of the question. For Freud, these were anxious times in other ways: all three of his sons were in the army, two of them almost daily in mortal danger.

Yet the war did not idle Freud's mind. Having too much time on his hands, he used it to good purpose. Work was a defense against brooding. Between March and July 1915, he wrote a dozen fundamental papers on metapsychology—on the unconscious, on repression, on melancholia; but he refused to gather them into the basic textbook he had planned. He published five of the papers between 1915 and 1917, and destroyed the rest. His enigmatic dissatisfaction with them hints at the discontent that had fueled his paper on narcissism. His map of the mind was inadequate to the evidence he had accumulated in his clinical experience. But he still lacked a satisfactory alternative. That would have to wait until after the war.

Another wartime activity, though more successful, gave Freud only modest pleasure: beginning in 1915, he delivered lectures at the university, published as a single volume in 1917 as *Introductory Lectures on Psycho-Analysis*. With the cunning of the born popularizer, Freud opened with a series on ordinary experiences, slips of the tongue, "unmotivated" forgetting, then turned to dreams and concluded with the technical topic, neuroses. Frequently reprinted and widely translated, these *Introductory Lectures* finally secured Freud a wide audience.

The war dragged on. Originally, somewhat to his surprise, an Austrian patriot, Freud wearied of the endless slaughter. He grew appalled at the chauvinism of intellectuals, the callousness of commanders, the stupidity of politicians. He had not yet fully acknowledged the theoretical significance of aggression, even though psychoanalysts had regularly encountered aggressiveness among their patients. But the war, beastly as it was, confirmed the skeptical psychoanalytic appraisal of human nature.

Signs of revived activity came shortly before the end of hostilities. In September 1918, for the first time since 1913, psychoanalysts from Germany and Austria-Hungary met in Budapest. Two months later, the war was over. To the family's immense relief, all of Freud's sons survived it. But the time for worry was far from over. The defeated powers were faced with revolution, drastically transformed from empires into republics, and saddled with stringent, vindictive peace treaties stripping them of territory and resources. Vienna was hungry, cold, desperate; food and fuel shortages produced deadly ailments—tuberculosis and influenza. In this stressful situation, Freud, who wasted no tears on the departed Hapsburg Empire, proved an energetic, imaginative manager. The portrait of Martha Freud shielding Herr Professor from domestic realities needs revision. Freud dispatched precise requests abroad to relatives, friends, associates, specifying what nourishment and clothing his family needed most, and how to send packages safely. Then, in January 1920, postwar misery struck home with deadly force: Freud's beloved second daughter Sophie, married and living in Hamburg, mother of two children, died in the influenza epidemic.

It has been plausibly argued that her death suggested the pessimistic drive theory that Freud now developed. Actually, he had virtually completed *Beyond the Pleasure Principle* (1920), which first announced Freud's theory of the death drive, the year before. Once Freud had adopted this construct, in which the forces of life, Eros, dramatically confront the forces of death, Thanatos, he found himself unable to think any other way. In 1923, in his classic study *The Ego and the Id*, he completed his revisions. He now proposed a "structural theory" of the mind, which visualizes the mind as divided into three distinct yet interacting agencies: the id (the wholly unconscious domain of the mind, consisting of the drives and of material later repressed), the ego (which is partly conscious and contains the defense mechanisms and the capacities to calculate, reason, and plan), and the super-ego (also only partly conscious, which harbors the conscience and, beyond that, unconscious feelings of guilt). This new scheme did not lead Freud to abandon his classic characterization of mental activity—emphasizing the distance of thoughts from awareness—as either conscious, or preconscious, or wholly unconscious. But he now made the decisive point that many of the mental operations of the ego, and of the super-ego as well, are inaccessible to direct introspection.

Meanwhile, the psychoanalytic movement was flourishing. Freud was becoming a household word, though he detested the sensationalized attention the popular press gave him. Better: in 1920, at the first postwar congress at The Hague, former "enemies" met as friends. Freud was accompanied by his daughter Anna, whom he was then analyzing and who joined the Vienna Psychoanalytic Society in 1922. In that year, the analysts convened in Berlin. It was the last congress Freud ever attended. In April 1923, he was operated on for a growth in his palate. While for months his doctors and closest associates pretended that the growth was benign, by September the truth was out: he had cancer. Severe operations followed in the fall. From then on Freud, compelled to wear a prosthesis, was rarely free of discomfort or pain.

But he never stopped working. While he had trouble speaking, he continued to analyze patients, many of them American physicians who came to Vienna as his "pupils" and returned to analyze in New York or Chicago. He continued to revise his theories. From the mid-1920s on, he wrote controversial papers on female sexuality and, in 1926, *Inhibitions, Symptoms, and Anxiety,* which reversed his earlier thinking on anxiety, now treating it as a danger signal. Moreover, he wrote essays that found a relatively wide public: *The Future of an Illusion,* a convinced atheist's dissection of religion, in 1927, and, in 1930, *Civilization and Its Discontents,* a disillusioned look at modern civilization on the verge of catastrophe.

In 1933, that catastrophe came. On January 30, Hitler was appointed chancellor in Germany, and from then on

Austrian Nazis, already active, increasingly intervened in politics. The old guard was disappearing: Karl Abraham had died prematurely in 1925; Sandor Ferenczi followed him in 1933. Freud's closest friends were gone. But Freud was unwilling to leave the Vienna he hated and loved: he was too old, he did not want to desert, and besides, the Nazis would never invade his country. On the morning of March 12, 1938, the Germans proved him wrong. As the Nazis marched in, a jubilant populace greeted them. Spontaneous anti-Semitic outrages surpassed anything Germans had witnessed after five years of Nazi rule. Late in March, Anna was summoned to Gestapo headquarters; while she was released unharmed, the trauma changed Freud's mind: he must emigrate. It took months to satisfy the Nazi government's extortions, but on June 4, Freud left for Paris, welcomed by his former analysand and loving disciple, Princess Marie Bonaparte. On June 6, Freud landed in London, preceded by most of his family, "to die in freedom."

Aged and ill, he kept on working. Freud's last completed book, *Moses and Monotheism,* irritated and dismayed his Jewish readers with its assertion that Moses had been an Egyptian: he ended life as he had lived it—a disturber of the peace. He died bravely on September 23, 1939, asking his physician for a lethal dose of morphine. Freud did not believe in personal immortality, but his work lives on.

ABOUT THIS BOOK

There were three or four occasions in his career as a psychoanalytic theoretician when Freud changed his mind on fundamental issues. *Inhibitions, Symptoms and Anxiety,* pub-

lished in 1926 but gestating for some time, is evidence for
one of them. The immediate cause of Freud's rethinking of
anxiety—despite its title the main subject of the book—was
the defection of his young friend, amaneunsis, and, until the
early 1920s, wholly loyal follower Otto Rank, who argued
that one anxiety, that experienced at birth, was the only
cause of anxiety that really mattered. Freud disagreed, and
Inhibitions, Symptoms and Anxiety was the result. Freud
saw several types of anxiety at work in the mind, most of
them appropriate to a certain stage in life, some rational and
some neurotic, some fleeting and some lifelong. What is
more, while in the theory he abandoned Freud had argued
that repression causes anxiety, he now reversed the field to
assert that anxiety causes repression. There is far more to his
new theory of anxiety than this, and the book repays—
indeed requires—careful reading. For both its flat enumera-
tive title and its rather disheveled mode of presentation,
quite untypical of his usual procedure, partially conceal the
clinical and theoretical riches of the book.

EDITOR'S INTRODUCTION
Hemmung, Symptom und Angst

(a) GERMAN EDITIONS:

1926   Leipzig, Vienna and Zurich: Internationaler Psychoanalytischer Verlag. Pp. 136.

1928   *G.S.*, 11, 23-115.

1931   *Neurosenlehre und Technik*, 205-99.

1948   *G.W.*, 14, 113-205.

(b) ENGLISH TRANSLATIONS:
Inhibition, Symptom and Anxiety

1927   Stamford, Conn.: Psychoanalytic Institute. Pp. vi + 103. (Tr. supervised L. Pierce Clark; Pref. S. Ferenczi.)

Inhibitions, Symptoms and Anxiety

1935–6   *Psychoanal. Quart.*, 4 (4), 616–25; 5 (1), 1–28; (2) 261–79; (3) 415–43. (Tr. H. A. Bunker.)

The Problem of Anxiety

1936   New York: Psychoanalytic Quarterly Press and W. W. Norton. Pp. vii + 165. (The above reprinted in volume form.)

Inhibitions, Symptoms and Anxiety

1936   London: Hogarth Press and Institute of Psycho-Analysis. Pp. 179. (Tr. Alix Strachey.)

An extract from Chapter I of the original appeared in the Vienna *Neue Freie Presse* of February 21, 1926. A part of the first American translation was reprinted in the *Archives of Psychoanalysis*, 1 (1927), 461–521. All three of the translations were authorized by Freud, and, as Ernest Jones points out (1957, 139–40), the translators of the last two prepared their work simultaneously, and in complete ignorance of each other's activities.

The present translation is a considerably modified version of the one published in London in 1936.

We learn from Ernest Jones that this book was written in July, 1925, and that it was revised in December of the same year and published in the third week of the following February.

The topics with which it deals range over a wide field, and there are signs that Freud found an unusual difficulty in unifying the work. This is shown, for instance, in the way in which the same subject often comes up for discussion at more than one point in very similar terms, in the necessity under which Freud found himself of tidying up a number of separate questions in his 'Addenda', and even in the actual title of the book. It is nevertheless true that—in spite of such important side-issues as the different classes of resistance, the distinction between repression and defence, and the relations between anxiety, pain and mourning—the problem of anxiety is its main theme. A glance at the list given in Appendix B (p. 113 below) will be enough to show how constantly present it was to Freud's mind from the beginning to the end of his psychological studies. Though on some aspects of the subject his opinions underwent little modification, on others, as he tells us in these pages, they were considerably altered. It will perhaps be of interest to trace, if only roughly, the history of these changes in two or three of the more important issues involved.

(a) Anxiety as Transformed Libido

It was in the course of investigating the 'actual' neuroses that Freud first came upon the problem of anxiety, and his earliest discussions of it will be found in his first paper on the anxiety neurosis (1895b) and in the memorandum on the subject which he sent to Fliess a little earlier, probably in the summer of 1894 (Freud, 1950a, Draft E). At that time he was still largely under the influence of his neurological studies and he was deep in his attempt at expressing the data of psychology in physiological terms. In particular, following Fechner, he had taken as a fundamental postulate the 'principle of constancy', according to which there was an inherent tendency in the nervous system to reduce, or at least to keep constant, the amount of excitation present in it. When, therefore, he made the clinical discovery that in cases of anxiety neurosis it was always possible to discover some interference with the discharge of sexual tension, it was natural for him to conclude that the accumulated excitation was finding its way out in the transformed shape of anxiety. He regarded this as a purely physical process without any psychological determinants.

From the first the anxiety occurring in phobias or in obsessional neuroses raised a complication, for here the presence of psychological events could not be excluded. But, as regards the emergence of anxiety, the explanation remained the same. In these cases—in the psychoneuroses—the *reason* for the accumulation of undischarged excitation was a psychological one: repression. But what followed was the same as in the 'actual' neuroses: the accumulated excitation (or libido) was transformed directly into anxiety.

Some quotations will show how loyally Freud maintained this view. In 'Draft E' (*c.* 1894), referred to above, he wrote: 'Anxiety arises from a *transformation* of the accumulated tension.' In *The Interpretation of Dreams* (1900*a*): 'Anxiety is a libidinal impulse which has its origin in the unconscious and is inhibited by the preconscious.' (*Standard Ed.*, 4, 337–8.) In *Gradiva* (1907*a*): 'The anxiety in anxiety-dreams, like neurotic anxiety in general, . . . arises out of libido by the process of repression.' (*Standard Ed.*, 9, 60–1.) In the metapsychological paper on 'Repression' (1915*d*): After repression 'the quantitative position [of the instinctual impulse—i.e. its energy] has not vanished, but has been transformed into anxiety'. (*Standard Ed.*, 14, 155.) Finally, as late as in 1920, Freud added in a footnote to the fourth edition of the *Three Essays:* 'One of the most important results of psycho-analytic research is this discovery that neurotic anxiety arises out of libido, that it is a transformation of it, and that it is thus related to it in the same kind of way as vinegar is to wine.' (*Standard Ed.*, 7, 224.) It is curious to note, however, that at quite an early stage Freud seems to have been assailed by doubts on the subject. In a letter to Fliess of November 14, 1897 (Freud, 1950*a*, Letter 75), he remarks, without any apparent connection with the rest of what he has been writing about: 'I have decided, then, henceforth to regard as separate factors what causes libido and what causes anxiety.' No further evidence is anywhere to be found of this isolated recantation. In the work before us Freud gave up the theory he had held for so long. He no longer regarded anxiety as transformed libido, but as a reaction on a particular model to situations of danger. But even here he still maintained (p. 73) that it was very possible that in the case of the anxiety neurosis 'what finds discharge in the generating of anxiety is precisely the surplus of unutilized libido'. This last relic of the old theory was to be abandoned a few years later. In a passage near the end of his discussion of anxiety in Lecture XXXII of his *New Introductory Lectures* (1933*a*) he wrote that in the anxiety neurosis, too, the appearance of anxiety was a reaction to a traumatic situation: 'we shall no longer maintain that it is the libido itself that is turned into anxiety in such cases.'

(b) Realistic and Neurotic Anxiety

In spite of his theory that neurotic anxiety was merely transformed libido, Freud was from the first at pains to insist on the close relation between anxiety due to external and to instinctual dangers. In his first paper on the anxiety neurosis (1895*b*) he wrote: 'The psyche is overtaken by the affect of anxiety if it feels that it is incapable of dealing by an appropriate reaction with a task (a danger) approaching from outside. In neuroses it is overtaken by anxiety if it notices that it is incapable of allaying a (sexual) excitation that has arisen from within. Thus it behaves as though it were projecting this excitation to the outside. The affect [normal anxiety] and the corresponding neurosis stand in a firm relation to each other: the former is the reaction to an exogenous excitation and the latter to an analogous endogenous one.'

This position, especially in connection with phobias, was elaborated later in many of Freud's writings—for instance, in the metapsychological papers on 'Repression' (1915*d*) and 'The Unconscious' (1915*e*), *Standard Ed.*, 14, 155–7 and 182–4, and in Lecture XXV of the *Introductory Lectures*. But it was difficult to maintain the sameness of the anxiety in the two classes of case so long as the direct derivation of anxiety from libido was insisted upon for the 'actual' neuroses. With the abandonment of this view and with the new distinction between automatic anxiety and anxiety as a signal, the whole situation was clarified and there ceased to be any reason for seeing a generic difference between neurotic and realistic anxiety.

(c) The Traumatic Situation and Situations of Danger

It adds to the difficulties of this book that the distinction between anxiety as a direct and automatic reaction to a trauma and anxiety as a signal of the danger of the approach of such a trauma, although touched on at several earlier points, is only clinched in the very last chapter. (A later and shorter account, given in Lecture XXXII of the *New Introductory Lectures,* may perhaps be found easier to grasp.)

The fundamental determinant of automatic anxiety is the occurrence of a traumatic situation; and the essence of this is an experience of helplessness on the part of the ego in the face of an accumulation of excitation, whether of external or of internal origin, which cannot be dealt with (pp. 68 and 102–03). Anxiety 'as a signal' is the response of the ego to the threat of the occurrence of a traumatic situation. Such a threat constitutes a situation of danger. Internal dangers change with the period of life (pp. 79–80), but they have a common characteristic, namely that they involve separation from, or loss of, a loved object, or a loss of its love (p. 84)—a loss or separation which might in various ways lead to an accumulation of unsatisfied desires and so to a situation of helplessness. Though Freud had not brought all these factors together before, each of them has a long previous history.

The traumatic situation itself is clearly the direct descendant of the state of accumulated and undischarged tension in Freud's earliest writings on anxiety. Some of the accounts of it given here might be quotations from 1894 or 1895. For instance, 'suffering a pain which will not stop or experiencing an accumulation of instinctual needs which cannot obtain satisfaction' on p. 68 below may be compared with 'a psychical accumulation of excitation . . . due to discharge being held up', from 'Draft E' (Freud, 1950a). At this early period the accumulated excitations, it is true, were almost invariably thought of as libidinal, but not *quite* invariably. Later on in the same 'Draft E' is a sentence which points out that anxiety may be 'a sensation of an accumulation of another endogenous stimulus—the stimulus towards breathing . . .; anxiety may therefore be capable of being used in relation to accumulated physical tension in general'. Again, in the 'Project' of 1895 (Freud, 1950a, Part I, Section 1) Freud enumerates the major needs which give rise to endogenous stimuli calling for discharge—'hunger, respiration and sexuality', and in a later passage (Part I, Section 11) remarks that in some conditions this discharge 'requires an alteration in the external world (e.g. the supply of nourishment or the proximity of the sexual object)' which 'at early stages the human organism is incapable of achieving'. To bring this about 'extraneous help' is needed, which the child attracts by his screams. And here Freud comments on the 'original helplessness of human beings'. There is a similar reference in Part III, Section 1, of the same work to the necessity of 'attracting the attention of some helpful personage (who is usually the wished-for object itself) to the child's longing and distress'. These passages seem to be an early hint at the situation of helplessness described here (pp. 66–69), in which the infant misses his mother—a situation that had been clearly stated in the footnote to the *Three Essays*

(1905*d*) in which Freud explained a child's anxiety in the dark as being due to 'the absence of someone he loved' (*Standard Ed.*, 7, 224).

But this has taken us on to the question of the various specific dangers which are liable to precipitate a traumatic situation at different times of life. These are briefly: birth, loss of the mother as an object, loss of the penis, loss of the object's love, loss of the super-ego's love. The question of birth is dealt with in the next section and we have just mentioned some early references to the importance of separation from the mother. The danger of castration with its devastating effects is no doubt the most familiar of all these dangers. But it is worth recalling a footnote added in 1923 to the case history of 'Little Hans' (1909*b*), in which Freud deprecates the application of the name 'castration complex' to the other kinds of separation which the child must inevitably experience (*Standard Ed.*, 10, 8 *n.*). We may possibly see in that passage a first hint at the concept of anxiety due to separation which comes into prominence here. The stress laid on the danger of losing the love of the loved object is explicitly related (on p. 75) to the characteristics of female sexuality, which had only recently begun to occupy Freud's mind.[1] Finally, the danger of losing the love of the super-ego carries us back to the long-debated problems of the sense of guilt, which had been re-stated only shortly before in *The Ego and the Id* (1923*b*).

---

[1] In his papers on 'The Dissolution of the Oedipus Complex' (1924*d*) and on the physiological distinction between the sexes (1925*j*), Freud had begun to emphasize the differences between the sexual development of boys and girls and at the same time to insist on the fact that in both sexes the mother is the first love-object. The history of this shift of emphasis in his views will be found discussed in the Editor's Note to the second of these two papers.

(d) Anxiety as a Signal

As applied to unpleasure in general, this notion was a very old one of Freud's. In Section 6 of Part II of the posthumous 'Project' of 1895 (Freud, 1950*a*) there is an account of a mechanism by which the ego restricts the generation of painful experiences: 'In this way the release of unpleasure is restricted in quantity, and its start acts as a signal to the ego to set normal defence in operation.' Similarly in *The Interpretation of Dreams* (1900*a*), *Standard Ed.*, 5, 602, it is laid down that thinking must aim 'at restricting the development of affect in thought-activity to the minimum required for acting as a signal'. In 'The Unconscious' (1915*e*), *Standard Ed.*, 14, 183, the idea is already applied to anxiety. Discussing the appearance of 'substitutive ideas' in phobia, Freud writes: 'Excitation of any point in this outer structure must inevitably, on account of its connection with the substitutive idea, give rise to a slight development of anxiety; and this is now used as a signal to inhibit . . . the further progress of the development of anxiety.' Similarly in Lecture XXV of the *Introductory Lectures* the state of 'anxious expectancy' is described in one or two places as offering a 'signal' to prevent an outbreak of severe anxiety. From this it was not a long step to the illuminating exposition in these pages. It may be remarked that in the present work too the concept is first introduced as a signal of 'unpleasure' (p. 10) and only subsequently as one of 'anxiety'.

(e) Anxiety and Birth

There remains the question of what it is that determines the *form* in which anxiety is manifested. This, too, was discussed by Freud in his early writings. To begin with (consistently with his view of anxiety as transformed libido) he regarded the most striking of its symptoms—the breathlessness and palpitations—as elements in the act of copulation, which, in the absence of the normal means of discharging the excitation, made their appearance in an isolated and exaggerated shape. This account will be found in Draft E of the Fliess papers, referred to above, and probably dating from June 1894, and at the end of Section III of the first paper on anxiety neurosis (1895*b*); and it is repeated in the 'Dora' case history (1905*e* [1901]), where Freud wrote: 'I maintained years ago that the dyspnoea and palpitations that occur in hysteria and anxiety neurosis are only detached fragments of the act of copulation.' (*Standard Ed.*, 7, 80.) It is not clear how all this fitted in with Freud's views on the expression of the emotions in general. These seem certainly to have been ultimately derived from Darwin. In the *Studies on Hysteria* (1895*d*) he twice quoted Darwin's volume on the subject (Darwin, 1872), and on the second occasion recalled that Darwin has taught us that the expression of the emotions 'consists of actions which originally had a meaning and served a purpose' (*Standard Ed.*, 2, 181). In a discussion before the Vienna Psycho-Analytical Society in 1909, Freud is reported by Jones (1955, 494) as having said that 'every affect . . . is only a reminiscence of an event'. Much later, in Lecture XXV of the *Introductory Lectures* (1916–17), he took up this point again, and expressed his belief that the 'nucleus' of an affect is 'the repetition of some particular significant experience'. He recalled, too, the explanation he had earlier given of hysterical attacks (1909*a*, *Standard Ed.*, 9, 232) as revivals of events in infancy, and added his conclusion that 'a hysterical attack may be likened to a freshly constructed individual affect, and a normal effect to the expression of a general hysteria which has become a heritage'. He repeats this theory in almost the same terms in the present work (pp. 12 and 62–63).

Whatever part this theory of the affects played in Freud's *earlier* explanation of the form taken by anxiety, it played an essential one in his *new* explanation, which emerged, apparently without warning, in a footnote added to the second edition of *The Interpretation of Dreams* (*Standard Ed.*, 5, 400). At the end of some discussion of phantasies about life in the womb, he went on (and printed the sentence in spaced type): 'Moreover, the act of birth is the first experience of anxiety, and thus the source and prototype of the affect of anxiety.' The edition was published in 1909, but the preface is dated 'Summer 1908'. A possible clue to the sudden emergence at that moment of this revolutionary notion is to be found in the fact that Freud had only recently contributed a preface (dated 'March, 1908') to Stekel's book on anxiety states (Freud, 1908*f*). The preface, it is true, contains not the faintest hint at the new theory, while Stekel's book itself seems explicitly to accept Freud's earlier one of the connection between anxiety and copulation. Nonetheless, Freud's interest must no doubt have been focused once again on the problem, and it may be that at that point an old memory may have been revived of an event which he described later, in the course of his discussion of anxiety in the *Introductory Lectures*. This memory was of what had been intended as a comic anecdote, told to him when he was a house physician by another young doctor, of how a midwife had declared that there is a connection between birth and being frightened. The memory must have gone back to about 1884, though Freud seems not to have mentioned it till this lecture in 1917. It seems possible that it had in fact been stirred up by his reading of Stekel's book and had provoked the appearance of the new theory in 1908. Thereafter that theory was never dropped. He gave it special prominence in the first of his papers on the psychology of love (1910*h*), *Standard Ed.*, 11, 173. Though this was not published till 1910, we learn that the gist of it was given before the Vienna Psycho-Analytical Society in May, 1909; while in November of the same year the minutes of the society (quoted by Jones, 1955, 494) report him as having remarked that children begin their experience of anxiety in the act of birth itself.

After the lecture in 1917 the subject lay fallow for some years, till it suddenly re-appeared at the end of the last paragraph but two of *The Ego and the Id* (1923*b*), where Freud spoke of birth as 'the first great anxiety-state'. This carries us up to the time of the publication of Rank's book *The Trauma of Birth*. The chronological relation between this sentence of Freud's and Rank's book is not entirely clear. *The Ego and the Id* was published in April, 1923. The title-page of Rank's book bears the date '1924'; but on its last page appear the words 'written in April, 1923', and the dedication declares that the book was 'presented' to Freud on May 6, 1923 (Freud's birthday). Although Ernest Jones (1957, 60) says specifically that Freud had not read it before its publication in December, 1923, he had nevertheless been aware of the general line of Rank's ideas as early as in September, 1922 (ibid., 61), and this is no doubt enough to account for the reference to birth in *The Ego and the Id*.

Rank's book was far more than an adoption of Freud's explanation of the *form* taken by anxiety. He argued that all later attacks of anxiety were attempts at 'abreacting' the trauma of birth. He accounted for all neuroses on similar lines, incidentally dethroning the Oedipus complex, and proposed a reformed therapeutic technique based on the overcoming of the birth trauma. Freud's published references to the book seemed at first to be favourable.[2] But the present work shows a complete and final reversal of that opinion. His rejection of Rank's views, however, stimulated him to a reconsideration of his own, and *Inhibitions, Symptoms and Anxiety* was the result.

---

[2]See, for instance, a footnote added to the 'Little Hans' analysis in 1923 (*Standard Ed.*, 10, 116) and another added to the *Three Essays* at about the same date (ibid., 7, 226). A full account of Freud's fluctuating attitude appears in Jones, 1957, 61 ff.

INHIBITIONS, SYMPTOMS
AND ANXIETY

I

In the description of pathological phenomena, linguistic usage enables us to distinguish symptoms from inhibitions, without, however, attaching much importance to the distinction. Indeed, we might hardly think it worth while to differentiate exactly between the two, were it not for the fact that we meet with illnesses in which we observe the presence of inhibitions but not of symptoms and are curious to know the reason for this.

The two concepts are not upon the same plane. Inhibition has a special relation to function. It does not necessarily have a pathological implication. One can quite well call a normal restriction of a function an inhibition of it. A symptom, on the other hand, actually denotes the presence of some pathological process. Thus, an inhibition may be a symptom as well. Linguistic usage, then, employs the word *inhibition* when there is a simple lowering of function, and *symptom* when a function has undergone some unusual change or when a new phenomenon has arisen out of it. Very often it seems to be quite an arbitrary matter whether we emphasize the positive side of a pathological process and call its outcome a symptom, or its negative side and call its outcome an inhibition. But all this is really of little interest;

and the problem as we have stated it does not carry us very far.

Since the concept of inhibition is so intimately associated with that of function, it might be helpful to examine the various functions of the ego with a view to discovering the forms which any disturbance of those functions assumes in each of the different neurotic affections. Let us pick out for a comparative study of this kind the sexual function and those of eating, of locomotion and of professional work.

(a) The sexual function is liable to a great number of disturbances, most of which exhibit the characteristics of simple inhibitions. These are classed together as psychical impotence. The normal performance of the sexual function can only come about as the result of a very complicated process, and disturbances may appear at any point in it. In men the chief stages at which inhibition occurs are shown by: a turning away of the libido at the very beginning of the process (psychical-unpleasure); an absence of the physical preparation for it (lack of erection); an abridgement of the sexual act *(ejaculatio praecox)*, an occurrence which might equally well be regarded as a symptom; an arrest of the act before it has reached its natural conclusion (absence of ejaculation); or a non-appearance of the psychical outcome (lack of the feeling of pleasure in orgasm). Other disturbances arise from the sexual function becoming dependent on special conditions of a perverse or fetishist nature.

That there is a relationship between inhibition and anxiety is pretty evident. Some inhibitions obviously represent a relinquishment of a function because its exercise would produce anxiety. Many women are openly afraid of the sexual function. We class this anxiety under hysteria, just as we do the defensive symptom of disgust which, arising originally as a deferred reaction to the experiencing of a passive sexual act, appears later whenever the *idea* of such an act is presented. Furthermore, many obsessional acts turn out to be measures of precaution and security against sexual experiences and are thus of a phobic character.

This is not very illuminating. We can only note that disturbances of the sexual function are brought about by a great variety of means. (1) The libido may simply be turned away (this seems most readily to produce what we regard as an inhibition pure and simple); (2) the function may be less well carried out; (3) it may be hampered by having conditions attached to it, or modified by being diverted to other aims; (4) it may be prevented by security measures; (5) if it cannot be prevented from starting, it may be immediately interrupted by the appearance of anxiety; and (6), if it is nevertheless carried out, there may be a subsequent reaction of protest against it and an attempt to undo what has been done.

(b) The function of nutrition is most frequently disturbed by a disinclination to eat, brought about by a withdrawal of libido. An increase in the desire to eat is also a not uncommon thing. The compulsion to eat is attributed to a fear of starving; but this is a subject which has been but little studied. The symptom of vomiting is known to us as a hysterical defence against eating. Refusal to eat owing to anxiety is a concomitant of psychotic states (delusions of being poisoned).

(c) In some neurotic conditions locomotion is inhibited by a disinclination to walk or a weakness in walking. In hysteria there will be a paralysis of the motor apparatus, or this one special function of the apparatus will be abolished (abasia). Especially characteristic are the increased difficulties that appear in locomotion owing to the introduction of certain stipulations whose non-observance results in anxiety (phobia).

(d) In inhibition in work—a thing which we so often have to deal with as an isolated symptom in our therapeutic work—the subject feels a decrease in his pleasure in it or becomes less able to do it well; or he has certain reactions to it, like fatigue, giddiness or sickness, if he is obliged to go on with it. If he is a hysteric he will have to give up his work owing to the appearance of organic and functional paralyses which make it impossible for him to carry it on. If he is an obsessional neurotic he will be perpetually being distracted from his work or losing time over it through the introduction of delays and repetitions.

Our survey might be extended to other functions as well; but there would be nothing more to be learnt by doing so. For we should not penetrate below the surface of the phenomena presented to us. Let us then proceed to describe inhibition in such a way as to leave very little doubt about what is meant by it, and say that inhibition is the expression of a *restriction of an ego-function.* A restriction of this kind can itself have very different causes. Some of the mechanisms involved in this renunciation of function are well known to us, as is a certain general purpose which governs it.

This purpose is more easily recognizable in the *specific* inhibitions. Analysis shows that when activities like playing the piano, writing or even walking are subjected to neurotic inhibitions it is because the physical organs brought into play—the fingers or the legs—have become too strongly erotized. It has been discovered as a general fact that the ego-function of an organ is impaired if its erotogenicity—its sexual significance—is increased. It behaves, if I may be allowed a rather absurd analogy, like a maid-servant who refuses to go on cooking because her master has started a love-affair with her. As soon as writing, which entails making a liquid flow out of a tube on to a piece of white paper, assumes the significance of copulation, or as soon as walking becomes a symbolic substitute for treading upon the body of mother earth, both writing and walking are stopped because they represent the performance of a forbidden sexual act. The ego renounces these functions, which are within its sphere, in order not to have to undertake fresh measures of repression—*in order to avoid a conflict with the id.*

There are clearly also inhibitions which serve the purpose of self-punishment. This is often the case in inhibitions of professional activities. The ego is not allowed to carry on those activities, because they would bring success and gain, and these are things which the severe super-ego has forbidden. So the ego gives them up too, *in order to avoid coming into conflict with the super-ego.*

The more *generalized* inhibitions of the ego obey a different mechanism of a simple kind. When the ego is involved in a particularly difficult psychical task, as occurs in mourning, or when there is some tremendous suppression of affect or when a continual flood of sexual phantasies has to be kept down, it loses so much of the energy at its disposal that it has to cut down the expenditure of it at many points at once. It is in the position of a speculator whose money has become tied up in his various enterprises. I came across an instructive example of this kind of intense, though short-lived, general inhibition. The patient, an obsessional neurotic, used to be overcome by a paralysing fatigue which lasted for one or more days whenever something occurred which should obviously have thrown him into a rage. We have here a point from which it should be possible to reach an understanding of the condition of general inhibition which characterizes states of depression, including the gravest form of them, melancholia.

As regards inhibitions, then, we may say in conclusion

that they are restrictions of the functions of the ego which have been either imposed as a measure of precaution or brought about as a result of an impoverishment of energy; and we can see without difficulty in what respect an inhibition differs from a symptom: for a symptom cannot any longer be described as a process that takes place within, or acts upon, the ego.

II

_____

The main characteristics of the formation of symptoms have long since been studied and, I hope, established beyond dispute.[1] A symptom is a sign of, and a substitute for, an instinctual satisfaction which has remained in abeyance; it is a consequence of the process of repression. Repression proceeds from the ego when the latter—it may be at the behest of the superego—refuses to associate itself with an instinctual cathexis which has been aroused in the id. The ego is able by means of repression to keep the idea which is the vehicle of the reprehensible impulse from becoming conscious. Analysis shows that the idea often persists as an unconscious formation.

So far everything seems clear; but we soon come upon difficulties which have not as yet been solved. Up till now our account of what occurs in repression has laid great stress on this point of exclusion from consciousness.[2] But it has left other points open to uncertainty. One question that arose was, what happened to the instinctual impulse which had been activated in the id and which sought satisfaction?

_____

[1] [See, for instance, the *Three Essays* (1905*d*), *Standard Ed.*, 7, 164.]
[2] [Cf. 'Repression' (1915*d*), *Standard Ed.*, 14, 147.]

The answer was an indirect one. It was that owing to the process of repression the pleasure that would have been expected from satisfaction had been transformed into unpleasure. But we were then faced with the problem of how the satisfaction of an instinct could produce unpleasure. The whole matter can be clarified, I think, if we commit ourselves to the definite statement that as a result of repression the intended course of the excitatory process in the id does not occur at all; the ego succeeds in inhibiting or deflecting it. If this is so the problem of 'transformation of affect' under repression disappears.[3] At the same time this view implies a concession to the ego that it can exert a very extensive influence over processes in the id, and we shall have to find out in what way it is able to develop such surprising powers.

It seems to me that the ego obtains this influence in virtue of its intimate connections with the perceptual system—connections which, as we know, constitute its essence and provide the basis of its differentiation from the id. The function of this system, which we have called *Pcpt.-Cs.*, is bound up with the phenomenon of consciousness.[4] It receives excitations not only from outside but from within, and endeavours, by means of the sensations of pleasure and unpleasure which reach it from these quarters, to direct the course of mental events in accordance with the pleasure principle. We are very apt to think of the ego as powerless

---

[3][The problem goes back a very long way. See, for instance, a letter to Fliess of December 6, 1896 (Freud, 1950a, Letter 52). The question was discussed by Freud in the 'Dora' case history (1905e), *Standard Ed.*, 7, 28–9, where an Editor's footnote gives a number of other references to the subject. The present solution was indicated in a short footnote added by Freud in 1925 to *Beyond the Pleasure Principle* (1920g), *Standard Ed.*, 18, 11.]

[4][Cf. *Beyond the Pleasure Principle* (1920g), *Standard Ed.*, 18, 24.]

against the id; but when it is opposed to an instinctual process in the id it has only to give a *'signal of unpleasure'*[5] in order to attain its object with the aid of that almost omnipotent institution, the pleasure principle. To take this situation by itself for a moment, we can illustrate it by an example from another field. Let us imagine a country in which a certain small faction objects to a proposed measure the passage of which would have the support of the masses. This minority obtains command of the press and by its help manipulates the supreme arbiter, 'public opinion', and so succeeds in preventing the measure from being passed.

But this explanation opens up fresh problems. Where does the energy come from which is employed for giving the signal of unpleasure? Here we may be assisted by the idea that a defence against an unwelcome *internal* process will be modelled upon the defence adopted against an *external* stimulus, that the ego wards off internal and external dangers alike along identical lines. In the case of external danger the organism has recourse to attempts at flight. The first thing it does is to withdraw cathexis from the perception of the dangerous object; later on it discovers that it is a better plan to perform muscular movements of such a sort as will render perception of the dangerous object impossible even in the absence of any refusal to perceive it—that it is a better plan, that is, to remove itself from the sphere of danger. Repression is an equivalent of this attempt at flight. The ego withdraws its (preconscious) cathexis from the instinctual representative[6] that is to be repressed and uses that cathexis for the purpose of releasing unpleasure (anxiety). The prob-

---

[5] [See Editor's Introduction, p. xxxiii.]

[6] [I.e. what represents the instinct in the mind. This term is fully discussed in the Editor's Note to 'Instincts and their Vicissitudes' (1915*c*), *Standard Ed.*, 14, 111 ff.]

lem of how anxiety arises in connection with repression may be no simple one; but we may legitimately hold firmly to the idea that the ego is the actual seat of anxiety and give up our earlier view that the cathectic energy of the repressed impulse is automatically turned into anxiety. If I expressed myself earlier in the latter sense, I was giving a phenomenological description and not a metapsychological account of what was occurring.

This brings us to a further question: how is it possible, from an economic point of view, for a mere process of withdrawal and discharge, like the withdrawing of a preconscious ego-cathexis, to produce unpleasure or anxiety, seeing that, according to our assumptions, unpleasure and anxiety can only arise as a result of an *increase* in cathexis? The reply is that this causal sequence should not be explained from an economic point of view. Anxiety is not newly created in repression; it is reproduced as an affective state in accordance with an already existing mnemic image. If we go further and enquire into the origin of that anxiety—and of affects in general—we shall be leaving the realm of pure psychology and entering the borderland of physiology. Affective states have become incorporated in the mind as precipitates of primaeval traumatic experiences, and when a similar situation occurs they are revived like mnemic symbols.[7] I do not think I have been wrong in likening them to the more recent and individually acquired hysterical attack and in regarding them as its normal prototypes.[8] In man and the higher animals it would seem that the act of birth, as the individual's first experience of anxiety, has given the affect

---

[7][This term was used by Freud throughout the *Studies on Hysteria* (1895*d*) in explaining hysterical symptoms. See, for instance, *Standard Ed.*, **2**, 297. A very clear account of the concept will be found in the first of the *Five Lectures* (1910*a*), *Standard Ed.*, **11**, 16 f.]

[8][See the Editor's Introduction, p. 35 and also below, p. 63.]

of anxiety certain characteristic forms of expression. But, while acknowledging this connection, we must not lay undue stress on it nor overlook the fact that biological necessity demands that a situation of danger should have an affective symbol, so that a symbol of this kind would have to be created in any case. Moreover, I do not think that we are justified in assuming that whenever there is an outbreak of anxiety something like a reproduction of the situation of birth goes on in the mind. It is not even certain whether hysterical attacks, though they were originally traumatic reproductions of this sort, retain that character permanently.

As I have shown elsewhere, most of the repressions with which we have to deal in our therapeutic work are cases of *after-*pressure.[9] They presuppose the operation of earlier, *primal repressions* which exert an attraction on the more recent situation. Far too little is known as yet about the background and preliminary stages of repression. There is a danger of overestimating the part played in repression by the super-ego. We cannot at present say whether it is perhaps the emergence of the super-ego which provides the line of demarcation between primal repression and after-pressure. At any rate, the earliest outbreaks of anxiety, which are of a very intense kind, occur before the super-ego has become differentiated. It is highly probable that the immediate precipitating causes of primal repressions are quantitative factors such as an excessive degree of excitation and the breaking through of the protective shield against stimuli.[10]

This mention of the protective shield sounds a note which recalls to us the fact that repression occurs in two different situations—namely, when an undesirable instinctual im-

---

[9][See 'Repression' (1915*d*), *Standard Ed.*, 14, 148.]
[10][Cf. *Beyond the Pleasure Principle* (1920*g*), *Standard Ed.*, 18, 27 ff.]

pulse is aroused by some external perception, and when it arises internally without any such provocation. We shall return to this difference later [p. 90]. But the protective shield exists only in regard to external stimuli, not in regard to internal instinctual demands.

So long as we direct our attention to the ego's attempt at flight we shall get no nearer to the subject of symptom-formation. A symptom arises from an instinctual impulse which has been detrimentally affected by repression. If the ego, by making use of the signal of unpleasure, attains its object of completely suppressing the instinctual impulse, we learn nothing of how this has happened. We can only find out about it from those cases in which repression must be described as having to a greater or less extent failed. In this event the position, generally speaking, is that the instinctual impulse has found a substitute in spite of repression, but a substitute which is very much reduced, displaced and inhibited and which is no longer recognizable as a satisfaction. And when the substitutive impulse is carried out there is no sensation of pleasure; its carrying out has, instead, the quality of a compulsion.

In thus degrading a process of satisfaction to a symptom, repression displays its power in a further respect. The substitutive process is prevented, if possible, from finding discharge through motility; and even if this cannot be done, the process is forced to expend itself in making alterations in the subject's own body and is not permitted to impinge upon the external world. It must not be transformed into action. For, as we know, in repression the ego is operating under the influence of external reality and therefore it debars the substitutive process from having any effect upon that reality.

Just as the ego controls the path to action in regard to the external world, so it controls access to consciousness. In repression it exercises its power in both directions, acting in the one manner upon the instinctual impulse itself and in the other upon the [psychical] representative of that impulse. At this point it is relevant to ask how I can reconcile this acknowledgement of the might of the ego with the description of its position which I gave in *The Ego and the Id.* In that book I drew a picture of its dependent relationship to the id and to the superego and revealed how powerless and apprehensive it was in regard to both and with what an effort it maintained its show of superiority over them.[11] This view has been widely echoed in psycho-analytic literature. Many writers have laid much stress on the weakness of the ego in relation to the id and of our rational elements in the face of the daemonic forces within us; and they display a strong tendency to make what I have said into a cornerstone of a psycho-analytic *Weltanschauung.* Yet surely the psycho-analyst, with his knowledge of the way in which repression works, should, of all people, be restrained from adopting such an extreme and one-sided view.

I must confess that I am not at all partial to the fabrication of *Weltanschauungen.*[12] Such activities may be left to philosophers, who avowedly find it impossible to make their journey through life without a Baedeker of that kind to give them information on every subject. Let us humbly accept the contempt with which they look down on us from the vantage-ground of their superior needs. But since *we* cannot forgo our narcissistic pride either, we will draw comfort from the reflection that such 'Handbooks to Life' soon grow out of date and that it is precisely our short-sighted, narrow and finicky work which obliges them to appear in new editions,

---

[11][*The Ego and the Id* (1923*b*), Chapter V.]
[12][Cf. a prolonged discussion of this in the last of Freud's *New Introductory Lectures* (1933*a*).]

and that even the most up-to-date of them are nothing but attempts to find a substitute for the ancient, useful and all-sufficient Church Catechism. We know well enough how little light science has so far been able to throw on the problems that surround us. But however much ado the philosophers may make, they cannot alter the situation. Only patient, persevering research, in which everything is subordinated to the one requirement of certainty, can gradually bring about a change. The benighted traveller may sing aloud in the dark to deny his own fears; but, for all that, he will not see an inch further beyond his nose.

III

To return to the problem of the ego.[1] The apparent contradiction is due to our having taken abstractions too rigidly and attended exclusively now to the one side and now to the other of what is in fact a complicated state of affairs. We were justified, I think, in dividing the ego from the id, for there are certain considerations which necessitate that step. On the other hand the ego is identical with the id, and is merely a specially differentiated part of it. If we think of this part by itself in contradistinction to the whole, or if a real split has occurred between the two, the weakness of the ego becomes apparent. But if the ego remains bound up with the id and indistinguishable from it, then it displays its strength. The same is true of the relation between the ego and the super-ego. In many situations the two are merged; and as a rule we can only distinguish one from the other when there is a tension or conflict between them. In repression the decisive fact is that the ego is an organization and the id is not. The ego is, indeed, the organized portion of the id. We should be quite wrong if we pictured the ego and the id as two opposing camps and if we supposed that, when the ego tries to suppress a part of the id by means of repression, the

---

[1] [I.e. the contrast between its strength and weakness in relation to the id.]

remainder of the id comes to the rescue of the endangered part and measures its strength with the ego. This may often be what happens, but it is certainly not the initial situation in repression. As a rule the instinctual impulse which is to be repressed remains isolated. Although the act of repression demonstrates the strength of the ego, in one particular it reveals the ego's powerlessness and how impervious to influence are the separate instinctual impulses of the id. For the mental process which has been turned into a symptom owing to repression now maintains its existence outside the organization of the ego and independently of it. Indeed, it is not that process alone but all its derivatives which enjoy, as it were, this same privilege of extra-territoriality; and whenever they come into associative contact with a part of the ego-organization, it is not at all certain that they will not draw that part over to themselves and thus enlarge themselves at the expense of the ego. An analogy with which we have long been familiar compared a symptom to a foreign body which was keeping up a constant succession of stimuli and reactions in the tissue in which it was embedded.[2] It does sometimes happen that the defensive struggle against an unwelcome instinctual impulse is brought to an end with the formation of a symptom. As far as can be seen, this is most often possible in hysterical conversion. But usually the outcome is different. The initial act of repression is followed by a tedious or interminable sequel in which the struggle against the instinctual impulse is prolonged into a struggle against the symptom.

In this secondary defensive struggle the ego presents two faces with contradictory expressions. The one line of behav-

---

[2][This analogy is discussed and criticized in Freud's contribution to *Studies on Hysteria* (1895*d*), *Standard Ed.*, **2**, 290–1 It appeared originally in the 'Preliminary Communication' (1893*a*), ibid., 6.]

iour it adopts springs from the fact that its very nature obliges it to make what must be regarded as an attempt at restoration or reconciliation. The ego is an organization. It is based on the maintenance of free intercourse and of the possibility of reciprocal influence between all its parts. Its desexualized energy still shows traces of its origin in its impulsion to bind together and unify, and this necessity to synthesize grows stronger in proportion as the strength of the ego increases. It is therefore only natural that the ego should try to prevent symptoms from remaining isolated and alien by using every possible method to bind them to itself in one way or another, and to incorporate them into its organization by means of those bonds. As we know, a tendency of this kind is already operative in the very act of forming a symptom. A classical instance of this are those hysterical symptoms which have been shown to be a compromise between the need for satisfaction and the need for punishment.[3] Such symptoms participate in the ego from the very beginning, since they fulfil a requirement of the super-ego, while on the other hand they represent positions occupied by the repressed and points at which an irruption has been made by it into the ego-organization. They are a kind of frontier-station with a mixed garrison.[4] (Whether all primary hysterical symptoms are constructed on these lines would be worth enquiring into very carefully.) The ego now proceeds to behave as though it recognized that the symptom had come to stay and that the only thing to do was to accept the situation in good part and draw as much advantage from it as possible. It makes an adaptation to the symptom—to this piece of the internal world which is alien

---

[3] [This idea was foreshadowed in Section II of Freud's second paper on 'The Neuro-Psychoses of Defence' (1896*b*).]

[4] [There is an allusion in this metaphor to the fact that *'Besetzung'*, the German word for 'cathexis', can also have the sense of 'garrison'.]

to it—just as it normally does to the real external world. It can always find plenty of opportunities for doing so. The presence of a symptom may entail a certain impairment of capacity, and this can be exploited to appease some demand on the part of the super-ego or to refuse some claim from the external world. In this way the symptom gradually comes to be the representative of important interests; it is found to be useful in asserting the position of the self and becomes more and more closely merged with the ego and more and more indispensable to it. It is only very rarely that the physical process of 'healing' round a foreign body follows such a course as this. There is a danger, too, of exaggerating the importance of a secondary adaptation of this kind to a symptom, and of saying that the ego has created the symptom merely in order to enjoy its advantages. It would be equally true to say that a man who had lost his leg in the war had got it shot away so that he might thenceforward live on his pension without having to do any more work.

In obsessional neurosis and paranoia the forms which the symptoms assume become very valuable to the ego because they obtain for it, not certain advantages, but a narcissistic satisfaction which it would otherwise be without. The systems which the obsessional neurotic constructs flatter his self-love by making him feel that he is better than other people because he is specially cleanly or specially conscientious. The delusional constructions of the paranoic offer to his acute perceptive and imaginative powers a field of activity which he could not easily find elsewhere.

All of this results in what is familiar to us as the '(secondary) gain from illness' which follows a neurosis.[5] This gain comes to the assistance of the ego in its endeavour to incor-

---

[5][A full discussion of this was given in Lecture XXIV of the *Introductory Lectures* (1916–17).]

porate the symptom and increases the symptom's fixation. When the analyst tries subsequently to help the ego in its struggle against the symptom, he finds that these conciliatory bonds between ego and symptom operate on the side of the resistances and that they are not easy to loosen.

The two lines of behaviour which the ego adopts towards the symptom are in fact directly opposed to each other. For the other line is less friendly in character, since it continues in the direction of repression. Nevertheless the ego, it appears, cannot be accused of inconsistency. Being of a peaceable disposition it would like to incorporate the symptom and make it part of itself. It is from the symptom itself that the trouble comes. For the symptom, being the true substitute for and derivative of the repressed impulse, carries on the role of the latter; it continually renews its demands for satisfaction and thus obliges the ego in its turn to give the signal of unpleasure and put itself in a posture of defence.

The secondary defensive struggle against the symptom takes many shapes. It is fought out on different fields and makes use of a variety of methods. We shall not be able to say much about it until we have made an enquiry into the various different instances of symptom-formation. In doing this we shall have an opportunity of going into the problem of anxiety—a problem which has long been looming in the background. The wisest plan will be to start from the symptoms produced by the hysterical neurosis; for we are not as yet in a position to consider the conditions in which the symptoms of obsessional neurosis, paranoia and other neuroses are formed.

IV

————————

Let us start with an infantile hysterical phobia of animals—
for instance, the case of 'Little Hans' [1909b], whose phobia
of horses was undoubtedly typical in all its main features.
The first thing that becomes apparent is that in a concrete
case of neurotic illness the state of affairs is much more
complex than one would suppose so long as one was dealing
with abstractions. It takes a little time to find one's bearings
and to decide which the repressed impulse is, what substitutive symptom it has found and where the motive for repression lies.

'Little Hans' refused to go out into the street because he
was afraid of horses. This was the raw material of the case.
Which part of it constituted the symptom? Was it his
having the fear? Was it his choice of an object for his fear?
Was it his giving up of his freedom of movement? Or was
it more than one of these combined? What was the satisfaction which he renounced? And why did he have to renounce
it?

At a first glance one is tempted to reply that the case is
not so very obscure. 'Little Hans's' unaccountable fear of
horses was the symptom and his inability to go out into the
streets was an inhibition, a restriction which his ego had

imposed on itself so as not to arouse the anxiety-symptom. The second point is clearly correct; and in the discussion which follows I shall not concern myself any further with this inhibition. But as regards the alleged symptom, a superficial acquaintance with the case does not even disclose its true formulation. For further investigation shows that what he was suffering from was not a vague fear of horses but a quite definite apprehension that a horse was going to bite him.[1] This idea, indeed, was endeavouring to withdraw from consciousness and get itself replaced by an undefined phobia in which only the anxiety and its object still appeared. Was it perhaps this idea that was the nucleus of his symptom?

We shall not make any headway until we have reviewed the little boy's psychical situation as a whole as it came to light in the course of the analytic treatment. He was at the time in the jealous and hostile Oedipus attitude towards his father, whom nevertheless—except in so far as his mother was the cause of estrangement—he dearly loved. Here, then, we have a conflict due to ambivalence: a well-grounded love and a no less justifiable hatred directed towards one and the same person. 'Little Hans's' phobia must have been an attempt to solve this conflict. Conflicts of this kind due to ambivalence are very frequent and they can have another typical outcome, in which one of the two conflicting feelings (usually that of affection) becomes enormously intensified and the other vanishes. The exaggerated degree and compulsive character of the affection alone betray the fact that it is not the only one present but is continually on the alert to keep the opposite feeling under suppression, and enable us to postulate the operation of a process which we call repression by means of *reaction-formation* (in the ego). Cases like

---

[1] [*Standard Ed.*, 10, 24.]

'Little Hans's' show no traces of a reaction-formation of this kind. There are clearly different ways of egress from a conflict due to ambivalence.

Meanwhile we have been able to establish another point with certainty. The instinctual impulse which underwent repression in 'Little Hans' was a hostile one against his father. Proof of this was obtained in his analysis while the idea of the biting horse was being followed up. He had seen a horse fall down and he had also seen a playmate, with whom he was playing at horses, fall down and hurt himself.[2] Analysis justified the inference that he had a wishful impulse that his father should fall down and hurt himself as his playmate and the horse had done. Moreover, his attitude towards someone's departure on a certain occasion[3] makes it probable that his wish that his father should be out of the way also found less hesitating expression. But a wish of this sort is tantamount to an intention of putting one's father out of the way oneself—is tantamount, that is, to the murderous impulse of the Oedipus complex.

So far there seem to be no connecting links between 'Little Hans's' repressed instinctual impulse and the substitute for it which we suspect is to be seen in his phobia of horses. Let us simplify his psychical situation by setting on one side the infantile factor and the ambivalence. Let us imagine that he is a young servant who is in love with the mistress of the house and has received some tokens of her favour. He hates his master, who is more powerful than he is, and he would like to have him out of the way. It would then be eminently natural for him to dread his master's vengeance and to develop a fear of him—just as 'Little Hans' developed a phobia of horses. We cannot, therefore,

---

[2][*Standard Ed.*, 10, 50 and 82.]
[3][Ibid., 29.]

describe the fear belonging to this phobia as a symptom. If 'Little Hans', being in love with his mother, had shown fear of his father, we should have no right to say that he had a neurosis or a phobia. His emotional reaction would have been entirely comprehensible. What made it a neurosis was one thing alone: the replacement of his father by a horse. It is this displacement, then, which has a claim to be called a symptom, and which, incidentally, constitutes the alternative mechanism which enables a conflict due to ambivalence to be resolved without the aid of a reaction-formation. [Cf. above, pp. 23–24.] Such a displacement is made possible or facilitated at 'Little Hans's' early age because the inborn traces of totemic thought can still be easily revived. Children do not as yet recognize or, at any rate, lay such exaggerated stress upon the gulf that separates human beings from the animal world.[4] In their eyes the grown man, the object of their fear and admiration, still belongs to the same category as the big animal who has so many enviable attributes but against whom they have been warned because he may become dangerous. As we see, the conflict due to ambivalence is not dealt with in relation to one and the same person: it is circumvented, as it were, by one of the pair of conflicting impulses being directed to another person as a substitutive object.

So far everything is clear. But the analysis of 'Hans's' phobia has been a complete disappointment in one respect. The distortion which constituted the symptom-formation was not applied to the [psychical] representative (the ideational content) of the instinctual impulse that was to be repressed; it was applied to a quite different representative and one which only corresponded to a *reaction* to the dis-

---

[4][Cf. 'A Difficulty in the Path of Psycho-Analysis' (1917a), *Standard Ed.*, 17, 140.]

agreeable instinct. It would be more in accordance with
our expectations if 'Little Hans' had developed, instead of
a fear of horses, an inclination to ill-treat them and to beat
them or if he had expressed in plain terms a wish to see them
fall down or be hurt or even die in convulsions ('make a row
with their feet').[5] Something of the sort did in fact emerge
in his analysis, but it was not by any means in the forefront
of his neurosis. And, curiously enough, if he really had produced a hostility of this sort not against his father but
against horses as his main symptom, we should not have said
that he was suffering from a neurosis. There must be something wrong either with our view of repression or with our
definition of a symptom. One thing, of course, strikes us at
once: if 'Little Hans' had really behaved like that to horses,
it would mean that repression had in no way altered the
character of his objectionable and aggressive instinctual
impulse itself but only the object towards which it was
directed.

Undoubtedly there are cases in which this is all that
repression does. But more than this happened in the development of 'Little Hans's' phobia—how much more can be
guessed from a part of another analysis.

As we know, 'Little Hans' alleged that what he was afraid
of was that a horse would bite him. Now some time later I
was able to learn something about the origin of another
animal phobia. In this instance the dreaded animal was a
wolf; it, too, had the significance of a father-substitute. As
a boy the patient in question—a Russian whom I did not
analyse till he was in his twenties—had had a dream (whose
meaning was revealed in analysis) and, immediately after it,
had developed a fear of being devoured by a wolf, like the

---

[5][*Standard Ed.*, 10, 50.]

seven little goats in the fairy tale.[6] In the case of 'Little Hans' the ascertained fact that his father used to play at horses with him[7] doubtless determined his choice of a horse as his anxiety-animal. In the same way it appeared at least highly probable that the father of my Russian patient used, when playing with him, to pretend to be a wolf and jokingly threaten to gobble him up.[8] Since then I have come across a third instance. The patient was a young American who came to me for analysis. He did not, it is true, develop an animal phobia, but it is precisely because of this omission that his case helps to throw light upon the other two. As a child he had been sexually excited by a fantastic children's story which had been read aloud to him about an Arab chief who pursued a 'ginger-bread man'[9] so as to eat him up. He identified himself with this edible person, and the Arab chief was easily recognizable as a father-substitute. This phantasy formed the earliest substratum of his auto-erotic phantasies.

The idea of being devoured by the father is typical age-old childhood material. It has familiar parallels in mythology (e.g. the myth of Kronos) and in the animal kingdom. Yet in spite of this confirmation the idea is so strange to us that we can hardly credit its existence in a child. Nor do we know whether it really means what it seems to say, and we cannot understand how it can have become the subject of a phobia. Analytic observation supplies the requisite information. It shows that the idea of being devoured by the father gives expression, in a form that has undergone regressive degrada-

---

[6]'From the History of an Infantile Neurosis' (1918*b*) [*Standard Ed.*, 17, 29 ff.].

[7][*Standard Ed.*, 10, 126–7.]

[8][*Standard Ed.*, 17, 32.]

[9][In English in the original.]

tion, to a passive, tender impulse to be loved by him in a genital-erotic sense. Further investigation of the case history[10] leaves no doubt of the correctness of this explanation. The genital impulse, it is true, betrays no sign of its tender purpose when it is expressed in the language belonging to the superseded transitional phase between the oral and sadistic organizations of the libido. Is it, moreover, a question merely of the replacement of the [psychical] representative by a regressive form of expression or is it a question of a genuine regressive degradation of the genitally-directed impulse in the id? It is not at all easy to make certain. The case history of the Russian 'Wolf Man' gives very definite support to the second, more serious, view; for, from the time of the decisive dream onward, the boy became naughty, tormenting and sadistic, and soon afterwards developed a regular obsessional neurosis. At any rate, we can see that repression is not the only means which the ego can employ for the purpose of defence against an unwelcome instinctual impulse. If it succeeds in making an instinct regress, it will actually have done it more injury than it could have by repressing it. Sometimes, indeed, after forcing an instinct to regress in this way, it goes on to repress it.

The case of the 'Wolf Man' and the somewhat less complicated one of 'Little Hans' raise a number of further considerations. But we have already made two unexpected discoveries. There can be no doubt that the instinctual impulse which was repressed in both phobias was a hostile one against the father. One might say that that impulse had been repressed by the process of being transformed into its opposite.[11] Instead of aggressiveness on the part of the subject towards his father, there appeared aggressiveness (in

---

[10][Of the Russian patient.]

[11][Cf. 'Instincts and their Vicissitudes' (1915*c*), *Standard Ed.*, 14, 126 ff.]

the shape of revenge) on the part of his father towards the subject. Since this aggressiveness is in any case rooted in the sadistic phase of the libido, only a certain amount of degradation is needed to reduce it to the oral stage. This stage, while only hinted at in 'Little Hans's' fear of being bitten, was blatantly exhibited in the 'Wolf Man's' terror of being devoured. But, besides this, the analysis has demonstrated, beyond a shadow of doubt, the presence of another instinctual impulse of an opposite nature which had succumbed to repression. This was a tender, passive impulse directed towards the father, which had already reached the genital (phallic) level of libidinal organization. As regards the final outcome of the process of repression, this impulse seems, indeed, to have been the more important of the two; it underwent a more far-reaching regression and had a decisive influence upon the content of the phobia. In following up a *single* instinctual repression we have thus had to recognize a convergence of *two* such processes. The two instinctual impulses that have been overtaken by repression—sadistic aggressiveness towards the father and a tender passive attitude to him—form a pair of opposites. Furthermore, a full appreciation of 'Little Hans's' case shows that the formation of his phobia had had the effect of abolishing his affectionate object-cathexis of his mother as well, though the actual content of his phobia betrayed no sign of this. The process of repression had attacked almost all the components of his Oedipus complex—both his hostile and his tender impulses towards his father and his tender impulses towards his mother. In my Russian patient this state of affairs was much less obvious.

These are unwelcome complications, considering that we only set out to study simple cases of symptom-formation due to repression, and with that intention selected the earliest and, to all appearances, most transparent neuroses of childhood. Instead of a single repression we have found a collection of them and have become involved with regression into the bargain. Perhaps we have added to the confusion by treating the two cases of animal phobia at our disposal—'Little Hans' and the 'Wolf Man'—as though they were cast in the same mould. As a matter of fact, certain differences between them stand out. It is only with regard to 'Little Hans' that we can say with certainty that what his phobia disposed of were the two main impulses of the Oedipus complex—his aggressiveness towards his father and his overfondness for his mother. A tender feeling for his father was undoubtedly there too and played a part in repressing the opposite feeling; but we can prove neither that it was strong enough to draw repression upon itself nor that it disappeared afterwards. 'Hans' seems, in fact, to have been a normal boy with what is called a 'positive' Oedipus complex. It is possible that the factors which we do not find were actually at work in him, but we cannot demonstrate their existence. Even the most exhaustive analysis has gaps in its data and is insufficiently documented. In the case of the Russian the deficiency lies elsewhere. His attitude to female objects had been disturbed by an early seduction[12] and his passive, feminine side was strongly developed. The analysis of his wolf-dream revealed very little intentional aggressiveness towards his father, but it brought forward unmistakable proof that what repression overtook was his passive tender attitude to his father. In his case, too, the other factors may have been operative as well; but they were not in evidence. How is it that, in spite of these differences in the two cases, almost amounting to an antithesis, the final outcome—a phobia—was approximately the same? The answer must be sought in another quarter. I think it will be found in the second fact

---

[12] [*Standard Ed.*, 17, 20 ff.]

which emerges from our brief comparative examination. It seems to me that in both cases we can detect what the motive force of the repression was and can substantiate our view of its nature from the line of development which the two children subsequently pursued. This motive force was the same in both of them. It was the fear of impending castration. 'Little Hans' gave up his aggressiveness towards his father from fear of being castrated. His fear that a horse would bite him can, without any forcing, be given the full sense of a fear that a horse would bite off his genitals, would castrate him. But it was from fear of being castrated, too, that the little Russian relinquished his wish to be loved by his father, for he thought that a relation of that sort presupposed a sacrifice of his genitals—of the organ which distinguished him from a female. As we see, both forms of the Oedipus complex, the normal, active form and the inverted one, came to grief through the castration complex. The Russian boy's anxiety-idea of being devoured by a wolf contained, it is true, no suggestion of castration, for the oral regression it had undergone had removed it too far from the phallic stage. But the analysis of his dream rendered further proof superfluous. It was a triumph of repression that the form in which his phobia was expressed should no longer have contained any allusion to castration.

Here, then, is our unexpected finding: in both patients the motive force of the repression was fear of castration. The ideas contained in their anxiety—being bitten by a horse and being devoured by a wolf—were substitutes by distortion for the idea of being castrated by their father. This was the idea which had undergone repression. In the Russian boy the idea was an expression of a wish which was not able to subsist in the face of his masculine revolt; in 'Little Hans' it was the expression of a reaction in him which had turned his aggressiveness into its opposite. But the *affect* of anxiety,

which was the essence of the phobia, came, not from the
process of repression, not from the libidinal cathexes of the
repressed impulses, but from the repressing agency itself.
The anxiety belonging to the animal phobias was an untrans-
formed fear of castration. It was therefore a realistic fear,[13]
a fear of a danger which was actually impending or was
judged to be a real one. It was anxiety which produced
repression and not, as I formerly believed, repression which
produced anxiety.

It is no use denying the fact, though it is not pleasant to
recall it, that I have on many occasions asserted that in
repression the instinctual representative is distorted, displaced, and so on, while the libido belonging to the instinctual impulse is transformed into anxiety.[14] But now an examination of phobias, which should be best able to provide
confirmatory evidence, fails to bear out my assertion; it
seems, rather, to contradict it directly. The anxiety felt in
animal phobias is the ego's fear of castration; while the
anxiety felt in agoraphobia (a subject that has been less
thoroughly studied) seems to be its fear of sexual temptation—a fear which, after all, must be connected in its origins
with the fear of castration. As far as can be seen at present,
the majority of phobias go back to an anxiety of this kind
felt by the ego in regard to the demands of the libido. It is
always the ego's attitude of anxiety which is the primary
thing and which sets repression going. Anxiety never arises
from repressed libido. If I had contented myself earlier with

---

[13]['*Realangst*' in the German. The adjective 'realistic' has, throughout the
Standard Edition, been preferred to the impossible 'real' and to 'objective'
which has been used elsewhere, but which gives rise to evident ambiguities.
On the other hand, for '*Realgefahr*' we have 'real danger'.]

[14][See, for instance, Freud's paper on repression (1915d), *Standard Ed.*,
14, 155, where the case of the 'Wolf Man' is also considered. A further
discussion will be found in Addendum A*(b)*, p. 96 ff., as well as in the
Editor's Introduction, p. xxvii ff.]

saying that after the occurrence of repression a certain amount of anxiety appeared in place of the manifestation of libido that was to be expected, I should have nothing to retract to-day. The description would be correct; and there does undoubtedly exist a correspondence of the kind asserted between the strength of the impulse that has to be repressed and the intensity of the resultant anxiety. But I must admit that I thought I was giving more than a mere description. I believed I had put my finger on a metapsychological process of direct transformation of libido into anxiety. I can now no longer maintain this view. And, indeed, I found it impossible at the time to explain how a transformation of that kind was carried out.

It may be asked how I arrived at this idea of transformation in the first instance. It was while I was studying the 'actual neuroses', at a time when analysis was still a very long way from distinguishing between processes in the ego and processes in the id.[15] I found that outbreaks of anxiety and a general state of preparedness for anxiety were produced by certain sexual practices such as *coitus interruptus*, undischarged sexual excitation or enforced abstinence—that is, whenever sexual excitation was inhibited, arrested or deflected in its progress towards satisfaction. Since sexual excitation was an expression of libidinal instinctual impulses it did not seem too rash to assume that the libido was turned into anxiety through the agency of these disturbances. The observations which I made at the time still hold good. Moreover, it cannot be denied that the libido belonging to the id-processes is subjected to disturbance at the instigation of repression. It might still be true, therefore, that in repression anxiety is produced from the libidinal cathexis of the instinctual impulses. But how can we reconcile this conclusion with

---

[15][See Freud's first paper on anxiety neurosis (1895*b*).]

our other conclusion that the anxiety felt in phobias is an ego anxiety and arises in the ego, and that it does not proceed out of repression but, on the contrary, sets repression in motion? There seems to be a contradiction here which it is not at all a simple matter to solve. It will not be easy to reduce the two sources of anxiety to a single one. We might attempt to do so by supposing that, when coitus is disturbed or sexual excitation interrupted or abstinence enforced, the ego scents certain dangers to which it reacts with anxiety. But this takes us nowhere. On the other hand, our analysis of the phobias seems to admit of no correction. *Non liquet.* 16

16['It is not clear.' An old legal verdict used when the evidence was inconclusive; compare the Scottish 'not proven'.]

V

We set out to study the formation of symptoms and the secondary struggle waged by the ego against symptoms. But in picking on the phobias for this purpose we have clearly made an unlucky choice. The anxiety which predominates in the picture of these disorders is now seen as a complication which obscures the situation. There are plenty of neuroses which exhibit no anxiety whatever. True conversion hysteria is one of these. Even in its most severe symptoms no admixture of anxiety is found. This fact alone ought to warn us against making too close a connection between anxiety and symptom-formation. The phobias are so closely akin to conversion hysteria in every other respect that I have felt justified in classing them alongside of it under the name of 'anxiety hysteria'. But no one has as yet been able to say what it is that determines whether any given case shall take the form of a conversion hysteria or a phobia—has been able, that is to say, to establish what determines the generating of anxiety in hysteria.

The commonest symptoms of conversion hysteria— motor paralyses, contractures, involuntary actions or discharges, pains and hallucinations—are cathectic processes which are either permanently maintained or intermittent. But this puts fresh difficulties in the way. Not much is

actually known about these symptoms. Analysis can show
what the disturbed excitatory process is which the symptoms
replace. It usually turns out that they themselves have a
share in that process. It is as though the whole energy of the
process had been concentrated in this one part of it. For
instance, it will be found that the pains from which a patient
suffers were present in the situation in which the repression
occurred; or that his hallucination was, at that time, a perception; or that his motor paralysis is a defence against an
action which should have been performed in that situation
but was inhibited; or that his contracture is usually a displacement of an intended innervation of the muscles in
some other part of his body; or that his convulsions are the
expression of an outburst of affect which has been withdrawn from the normal control of the ego. The sensation of
unpleasure which accompanies the appearance of the symptoms varies in a striking degree. In chronic symptoms which
have been displaced on to motility, like paralyses and contractures, it is almost always entirely absent; the ego behaves
towards the symptoms as though it had nothing to do with
them. In intermittent symptoms and in those concerned
with the sensory sphere, sensations of unpleasure are as a
rule distinctly felt; and in symptoms of pain these may reach
an extreme degree. The picture presented is so manifold
that it is difficult to discover the factor which permits of all
these variations and yet allows a uniform explanation of
them. There is, moreover, little to be seen in conversion
hysteria of the ego's struggle against the symptom after it
has been formed. It is only when sensitivity to pain in some
part of the body constitutes the symptom that that symptom
is in a position to play a dual role. The symptom of pain will
appear no less regularly whenever the part of the body concerned is touched from outside than when the pathogenic
situation which it represents is associatively activated from

within; and the ego will take precautions to prevent the symptom from being aroused through external perceptions. Why the formation of symptoms in conversion hysteria should be such a peculiarly obscure thing I cannot tell; but the fact affords us a good reason for quitting such an unproductive field of enquiry without delay.

Let us turn to the obsessional neuroses in the hope of learning more about the formation of symptoms. The symptoms belonging to this neurosis fall, in general, into two groups, each having an opposite trend. They are either prohibitions, precautions and expiations—that is, negative in character—or they are, on the contrary, substitutive satisfactions which often appear in symbolic disguise. The negative, defensive group of symptoms is the older of the two; but as illness is prolonged, the satisfactions, which scoff at all defensive measures, gain the upper hand. The symptom-formation scores a triumph if it succeeds in combining the prohibition with satisfaction so that what was originally a defensive command or prohibition acquires the significance of a satisfaction as well; and in order to achieve this end it will often make use of the most ingenious associative paths. Such an achievement demonstrates the tendency of the ego to synthesize, which we have already observed [p. 19]. In extreme cases the patient manages to make most of his symptoms acquire, in addition to their original meaning, a directly contrary one. This is a tribute to the power of ambivalence, which, for some unknown reason, plays such a large part in obsessional neuroses. In the crudest instance the symptom is diphasic:[1] an action which carries out a certain injunction is immediately succeeded by another ac-

---

[1] [I.e. occurs in two instalments. Cf. a passage near the end of Lecture XIX of the *Introductory Lectures* (1916–17). See also below, p. 46.]

tion which stops or undoes the first one even if it does not go quite so far as to carry out its opposite.

Two impressions at once emerge from this brief survey of obsessional symptoms. The first is that a ceaseless struggle is being waged against the repressed, in which the repressing forces steadily lose ground; the second is that the ego and the super-ego have a specially large share in the formation of the symptoms.

Obsessional neurosis is unquestionably the most interesting and repaying subject of analytic research. But as a problem it has not yet been mastered. It must be confessed that, if we endeavour to penetrate more deeply into its nature, we still have to rely upon doubtful assumptions and unconfirmed suppositions. Obsessional neurosis originates, no doubt, in the same situation as hysteria, namely, the necessity of fending off the libidinal demands of the Oedipus complex. Indeed, every obsessional neurosis seems to have a substratum of hysterical symptoms that have been formed at a very early stage.[2] But it is subsequently shaped along quite different lines owing to a constitutional factor. The genital organization of the libido turns out to be feeble and insufficiently resistant, so that when the ego begins its defensive efforts the first thing it succeeds in doing is to throw back the genital organization (of the phallic phase), in whole or in part, to the earlier sadistic-anal level. This fact of regression is decisive for all that follows.

Another possibility has to be considered. Perhaps regression is the result not of a constitutional factor but of a time-factor. It may be that regression is rendered possible not because the genital organization of the libido is too

---

[2][See the beginning of Section II of Freud's second paper on 'The Neuro-Psychoses of Defence' (1896b). An example occurs in the 'Wolf Man' analysis (1918b), *Standard Ed.*, **17**, 75.]

feeble but because the opposition of the ego begins too early, while the sadistic phase is at its height. I am not prepared to express a definite opinion on this point, but I may say that analytic observation does not speak in favour of such an assumption. It shows rather that, by the time an obsessional neurosis is entered upon, the phallic stage has already been reached. Moreover, the onset of this neurosis belongs to a later time of life than that of hysteria—to the second period of childhood, after the latency period has set in. In a woman patient whose case I was able to study and who was overtaken by this disorder at a very late date, it became clear that the determining cause of her regression and of the emergence of her obsessional neurosis was a real occurrence through which her genital life, which had up till then been intact, lost all its value.[3]

As regards the metapsychological explanation of regression, I am inclined to find it in a 'defusion of instinct', in a detachment of the erotic components which, with the onset of the genital stage, had joined the destructive cathexes belonging to the sadistic phase.[4]

In enforcing regression, the ego scores its first success in its defensive struggle against the demands of the libido. (In this connection it is of advantage to distinguish the more general notion of 'defence' from 'repression'.[5] Repression is only one of the mechanisms which defence makes use of.) It is perhaps in obsessional cases more than in normal or hysterical ones that we can most clearly recognize that the motive force of defence is the castration complex and that

---

[3] See my paper on 'The Disposition to Obsessional Neurosis' (1913*i*) [*Standard Ed.*, **12**, 319 f.].
[4] [Towards the beginning of Chapter IV of *The Ego and the Id* (1923*b*), Freud had suggested that the advance from the sadistic-anal to the genital phase is conditioned by an accession of erotic components.]
[5] [This is discussed at length below, in Addendum A*(c)*, p. 98 f.]

what is being fended off are the trends of the Oedipus complex. We are at present dealing with the beginning of the latency period, a period which is characterized by the dissolution of the Oedipus complex, the creation or consolidation of the super-ego and the erection of ethical and aesthetic barriers in the ego. In obsessional neuroses these processes are carried further than is normal. In addition to the destruction of the Oedipus complex a regressive degradation of the libido takes place, the super-ego becomes exceptionally severe and unkind, and the ego, in obedience to the super-ego, produces strong reaction-formations in the shape of conscientiousness, pity and cleanliness. Implacable, though not always on that account successful, severity is shown in condemning the temptation to continue early infantile masturbation, which now attaches itself to regressive (sadistic-anal) ideas but which nevertheless represents the unsubjugated part of the phallic organization. There is an inherent contradiction about this state of affairs, in which, precisely in the interests of masculinity (that is to say, from fear of castration), every activity belonging to masculinity is stopped. But here, too, obsessional neurosis is only overdoing the normal method of getting rid of the Oedipus complex. We once more find here an illustration of the truth that every exaggeration contains the seed of its own undoing. For, under the guise of obsessional acts, the masturbation that has been suppressed approaches ever more closely to satisfaction.

The reaction-formations in the ego of the obsessional neurotic, which we recognize as exaggerations of normal character-formation, should be regarded, I think, as yet another mechanism of defence and placed alongside of regression and repression. They seem to be absent or very much weaker in hysteria. Looking back, we can now get an idea of what is peculiar to the defensive process in hysteria. It seems that in it the process is limited to repression alone. The ego turns away from the disagreeable instinctual impulse, leaves it to pursue its course in the unconscious, and takes no further part in its fortunes. This view cannot be absolutely correct, for we are acquainted with the case in which a hysterical symptom is at the same time a fulfilment of a penalty imposed by the super-ego; but it may describe a general characteristic of the behavior of the ego in hysteria.

We can either simply accept it as a fact that in obsessional neurosis a super-ego of this severe kind emerges, or we can take the regression of the libido as the fundamental characteristic of the affection and attempt to relate the severity of the super-ego to it. And indeed the super-ego, originating as it does from the id, cannot dissociate itself from the regression and defusion of instinct which have taken place there. We cannot be surprised if it becomes harsher, unkinder and more tormenting than where development has been normal.

The chief task during the latency period seems to be the fending-off of the temptation to masturbate. This struggle produces a series of symptoms which appear in a typical fashion in the most different individuals and which in general have the character of a ceremonial. It is a great pity that no one has as yet collected them and systematically analysed them. Being the earliest products of the neurosis they should best be able to shed light on the mechanisms employed in its symptom-formation. They already exhibit the features which will emerge so disastrously if a serious illness follows. They tend to become attached to activities (which would later be carried out almost automatically) such as going to sleep, washing, dressing and walking about; and they tend also to repetition and waste of time. Why this should be so is at present not at all clear; but the sublimation of anal-erotic components plays an unmistakable part in it.

The advent of puberty opens a decisive chapter in the history of an obsessional neurosis. The genital organization which has been broken off in childhood starts again with great vigour. But, as we know, the sexual development in childhood determines what direction this new start at puberty will take. Not only will the early aggressive impulses be re-awakened; but a greater or lesser proportion of the new libidinal impulses—in bad cases the whole of them—will have to follow the course prescribed for them by regression and will emerge as aggressive and destructive tendencies. In consequence of the erotic trends being disguised in this way and owing to the powerful reaction-formations in the ego, the struggle against sexuality will henceforward be carried on under the banner of ethical principles. The ego will recoil with astonishment from promptings to cruelty and violence which enter consciousness from the id, and it has no notion that in them it is combating erotic wishes, including some to which it would not otherwise have taken exception. The overstrict super-ego insists all the more strongly on the suppression of sexuality, since this has assumed such repellent forms. Thus in obsessional neurosis the conflict is aggravated in two directions: the defensive forces become more intolerant and the forces that are to be fended off become more intolerable. Both effects are due to a single factor, namely, regression of the libido.

A good deal of what has been said may be objected to on the ground that the unpleasant obsessive ideas are themselves quite conscious. But there is no doubt that before becoming conscious they have been through the process of repression. In most of them the actual wording of the aggressive instinctual impulse is altogether unknown to the ego, and it requires a good deal of analytic work to make it conscious. What does penetrate into consciousness is usually only a distorted substitute which is either of a vague, dream-like and indeterminate nature or so travestied as to be unrecognizable. Even where repression has not encroached upon the content of the aggressive impulse it has certainly got rid of its accompanying affective character. As a result, the aggressiveness appears to the ego not to be an impulsion but, as the patients themselves say, merely a 'thought' which awakens no feeling.[6] But the remarkable thing is that this is not the case. What happens is that the affect left out when the obsessional idea is perceived appears in a different place. The super-ego behaves as though repression had not occurred and as though it knew the real wording and full affective character of the aggressive impulse, and it treats the ego accordingly. The ego which, on the one hand, knows that it is innocent is obliged, on the other hand, to be aware of a sense of guilt and to carry a responsibility which it cannot account for. This state of affairs is, however, not so puzzling as it would seem at first sight. The behavior of the super-ego is perfectly intelligible, and the contradiction in the ego merely shows that it has shut out the id by means of repression while remaining fully accessible to the influence of the super-ego.[7] If it is asked why the ego does not also attempt to withdraw from the tormenting criticism of the super-ego, the answer is that it *does* manage to do so in a great number of instances. There are obsessional neuroses in which no sense of guilt whatever is present. In them, as far as can be seen, the ego has avoided becoming aware of it by instituting a fresh set of symptoms, penances or restrictions of a self-punishing kind. These symptoms, however,

---

[6][For all of this, see the 'Rat Man' case history (1909*d*), *Standard Ed.*, 10, 221 ff. and 167 *n.*]
[7]Cf. Theodor Reik, 1925, 51.

represent at the same time a satisfaction of masochistic impulses which, in their turn, have been reinforced by regression.

Obsessional neurosis presents such a vast multiplicity of phenomena that no efforts have yet succeeded in making a coherent synthesis of all its variations. All we can do is to pick out certain typical correlations; but there is always the risk that we may have overlooked other uniformities of a no less important kind.

I have already described the general tendency of symptom-formation in obsessional neurosis. It is to give ever greater room to substitutive satisfaction at the expense of frustration. Symptoms which once stood for a restriction of the ego come later on to represent satisfactions as well, thanks to the ego's inclination to synthesis, and it is quite clear that this second meaning gradually becomes the more important of the two. The result of this process, which approximates more and more to a complete failure of the original purpose of defence, is an extremely restricted ego which is reduced to seeking satisfaction in the symptoms. The displacement of the distribution of forces in favour of satisfaction may have the dreaded final outcome of paralysing the will of the ego, which in every decision it has to make is almost as strongly impelled from the one side as from the other. The over-acute conflict between id and super-ego which has dominated the illness from the very beginning may assume such extensive proportions that the ego, unable to carry out its office of mediator, can undertake nothing which is not drawn into the sphere of that conflict.

VI

In the course of these struggles we come across two activities of the ego which form symptoms and which deserve special attention because they are obviously surrogates of repression and therefore well calculated to illustrate its purpose and technique. The fact that such auxiliary and substitutive techniques emerge may argue that true repression has met with difficulties in its functioning. If one considers how much more the ego is the scene of action of symptom-formation in obsessional neurosis than it is in hysteria and with what tenacity the ego clings to its relations to reality and to consciousness, employing all its intellectual faculties to that end—and indeed how the very process of thinking becomes hypercathected and erotized—then one may perhaps come to a better understanding of these variations of repression.

The two techniques I refer to are *undoing what has been done* and *isolating*. [1] The first of these has a wide range of application and goes back very far. It is, as it were, negative magic, and endeavours, by means of motor symbolism, to

---

[1][Both these techniques are referred to in the 'Rat Man' analysis (1909*d*), *Standard Ed.*, 10, 235–6 and 243. The first of them, in German *'ungeschehenmachen'*, means literally 'making unhappened'.]

'blow away' not merely the *consequences* of some event (or experience or impression) but the event itself. I choose the term 'blow away' advisedly, so as to remind the reader of the part played by this technique not only in neuroses but in magical acts, popular customs and religious ceremonies as well. In obsessional neurosis the technique of undoing what has been done is first met with in the 'diphasic' symptoms [p. 37], in which one action is cancelled out by a second, so that it is as though neither action had taken place, whereas, in reality, both have. This aim of undoing is the second underlying motive of obsessional ceremonials, the first being to take precautions in order to prevent the occurrence or recurrence of some particular event. The difference between the two is easily seen: the precautionary measures are rational, while trying to get rid of something by 'making it not to have happened' is irrational and in the nature of magic. It is of course to be suspected that the latter is the earlier motive of the two and proceeds from the animistic attitude towards the environment. This endeavour to undo shades off into normal behaviour in the case in which a person decides to regard an event as not having happened.[2] But whereas he will take no direct steps against the event, and will simply pay no further attention to it or its consequences, the neurotic person will try to make the past itself non-existent. He will try to repress it by motor means. The same purpose may perhaps account for the obsession for *repeating* which is so frequently met with in this neurosis and the carrying out of which serves a number of contradictory intentions at once. When anything has not happened in the desired way it is undone by being repeated in a different way; and thereupon all the motives that exist for lingering over such repetitions come into play as well. As the

---

[2][In the original: 'as *"non arrivé"* '.]

neurosis proceeds, we often find that the endeavour to undo a traumatic experience is a motive of first-rate importance in the formation of symptoms. We thus unexpectedly discover a new, motor technique of defence, or (as we may say in this case with less inaccuracy) of repression.

The second of these techniques which we are setting out to describe for the first time, that of isolation, is peculiar to obsessional neurosis. It, too, takes place in the motor sphere. When something unpleasant has happened to the subject or when he himself has done something which has a significance for his neurosis, he interpolates an interval during which nothing further must happen—during which he must perceive nothing and do nothing.[3] This behavior, which seems strange at first sight, is soon seen to have a relation to repression. We know that in hysteria it is possible to cause a traumatic experience to be overtaken by amnesia. In obsessional neurosis this can often not be achieved: the experience is not forgotten, but, instead, it is deprived of its affect, and its associative connections are suppressed or interrupted so that it remains as though isolated and is not reproduced in the ordinary processes of thought. The effect of this isolation is the same as the effect of repression with amnesia. This technique, then, is reproduced in the isolations of obsessional neurosis; and it is at the same time given motor reinforcement for magical purposes. The elements that are held apart in this way are precisely those which belong together associatively. The motor isolation is meant to ensure an interruption of the connection in thought. The normal phenomenon of concentration provides a pretext for this kind of neurotic procedure: what seems to us important in the way of an impression or a piece of work must not be interfered with by the simultaneous claims of any other

---

[3][Cf. the 'Rat Man', ibid., 246.]

mental processes or activities. But even a normal person uses concentration to keep away not only what is irrelevant or unimportant, but, above all, what is unsuitable because it is contradictory. He is most disturbed by those elements which once belonged together but which have been torn apart in the course of his development—as, for instance, by manifestations of the ambivalence of his father-complex in his relation to God, or by impulses attached to his excretory organs in his emotions of love. Thus, in the normal course of things, the ego has a great deal of isolating work to do in its function of directing the current of thought. And, as we know, we are obliged, in carrying out our analytic technique, to train it to relinquish that function for the time being, eminently justified as it usually is.

We have all found by experience that it is especially difficult for an obsessional neurotic to carry out the fundamental rule of psycho-analysis. His ego is more watchful and makes sharper isolations, probably because of the high degree of tension due to conflict that exists between his superego and his id. While he is engaged in thinking, his ego has to keep off too much—the intrusion of unconscious phantasies and the manifestation of ambivalent trends. It must not relax, but is constantly prepared for a struggle. It fortifies this compulsion to concentrate and to isolate by the help of the magical acts of isolation which, in the form of symptoms, grow to be so noticeable and to have so much practical importance for the patient, but which are, of course, useless in themselves and are in the nature of ceremonials.

But in thus endeavouring to prevent associations and connections of thought, the ego is obeying one of the oldest and most fundamental commands of obsessional neurosis, the taboo on touching. If we ask ourselves why the avoidance of touching, contact or contagion should play such a large part in this neurosis and should become the subject-matter of complicated systems, the answer is that touching and physical contact are the immediate aim of the aggressive as well as the loving object-cathexes.[4] Eros desires contact because it strives to make the ego and the loved object one, to abolish all spatial barriers between them. But destructiveness, too, which (before the invention of long-range weapons) could only take effect at close quarters, must presuppose physical contact, a coming to grips. To 'touch' a woman has become a euphemism for using her as a sexual object. Not to 'touch' one's genitals is the phrase employed for forbidding auto-erotic satisfaction. Since obsessional neurosis begins by persecuting erotic touching and then, after regression has taken place, goes on to persecute touching in the guise of aggressiveness, it follows that nothing is so strongly proscribed in that illness as touching nor so well suited to become the central point of a system of prohibitions. But isolating is removing the possibility of contact; it is a method of withdrawing a thing from being touched in any way. And when a neurotic isolates an impression or an activity by interpolating an interval, he is letting it be understood symbolically that he will not allow his thoughts about that impression or activity to come into associative contact with other thoughts.

This is as far as our investigations into the formation of symptoms take us. It is hardly worth while summing them up, for the results they have yielded are scanty and incomplete and tell us scarcely anything that we do not already know. It would be fruitless to turn our attention to symptom-formation in other disorders besides phobias, conversion hysteria and obsessional neurosis, for too little is known

---

[4][Cf. several passages in the second essay in *Totem and Taboo* (1912–13), e.g. *Standard Ed.*, 13, 27 ff. and 73.]

about them. But in reviewing those three neuroses together we are brought up against a very serious problem the consideration of which can no longer be put off. All three have as their outcome the destruction of the Oedipus complex; and in all three the motive force of the ego's opposition is, we believe, the fear of castration. Yet it is only in the phobias that this fear comes to the surface and is acknowledged. What has become of it in the other two neuroses? How has the ego spared itself this fear? The problem becomes accentuated when we recall the possibility, already referred to, that anxiety arises directly, by a kind of fermentation, from a libidinal cathexis whose processes have been disturbed. Furthermore, is it absolutely certain that fear of castration is the only motive force of repression (or defence)? If we think of neuroses in women we are bound to doubt it. For though we can with certainty establish in them the presence of a castration *complex,* we can hardly speak with propriety of castration *anxiety* where castration has already taken place.

VII

Let us go back again to infantile phobias of animals; for, when all is said and done, we understand them better than any other cases. In animal phobias, then, the ego has to oppose a libidinal object-cathexis coming from the id—a cathexis that belongs either to the positive or the negative Oedipus complex—because it believes that to give way to it would entail the danger of castration. This question has already been discussed, but there still remains a doubtful point to clear up. In 'Little Hans's' case—that is, in the case of a positive Oedipus complex—was it his fondness for his mother or was it his aggressiveness towards his father which called out the defence by the ego? In practice it seems to make no difference, especially as each set of feelings implies the other; but the question has a theoretical interest, since it is only the feeling of affection for the mother which can count as a purely erotic one. The aggressive impulse flows mainly from the destructive instinct; and we have always believed that in a neurosis it is against the demands of the libido and not against those of any other instinct that the ego is defending itself. In point of fact we know that after 'Hans's' phobia had been formed, his tender attachment to his mother seemed to disappear, having been completely disposed of by repression, while the formation of the symptom (the substitutive formation) took place in relation to his aggressive impulses. In the 'Wolf Man' the situation was simpler. The impulse that was repressed—his feminine attitude towards his father—was a genuinely erotic one; and it was in relation to that impulse that the formation of his symptoms took place.

It is almost humiliating that, after working so long, we should still be having difficulty in understanding the most fundamental facts. But we have made up our minds to simplify nothing and to hide nothing. If we cannot see things clearly we will at least see clearly what the obscurities are. What is hampering us here is evidently some hitch in the development of our theory of the instincts. We began by tracing the organization of the libido through its successive stages—from the oral through the sadistic-anal to the genital—and in doing so placed all the components of the sexual instinct on the same footing. Later it appeared that sadism was the representative of another instinct, which was opposed to Eros. This new view, that the instincts fall into two groups, seems to explode the earlier construction of the successive stages of libidinal organization. But we do not have to break fresh ground in order to find a way out of the difficulty. The solution has been at hand for a long time and lies in the fact that what we are concerned with are scarcely ever pure instinctual impulses but mixtures in various proportions of the two groups of instincts. If this is so, there is no need to revise our view of the organizations of the libido. A sadistic cathexis of an object may also legitimately claim to be treated as a libidinal one; and an aggressive impulse against the father can just as well be subjected to repression as a tender impulse towards the mother. Nevertheless we shall bear in mind for future consideration the possibility that repression is a process which has a special relation to the *genital* organization of the libido and that the ego resorts to other methods of defence when it has to secure itself against the libido on other levels of organization. To continue: a case like 'Little Hans's' does not enable us to come to any clear conclusion. It is true that in him an aggressive impulse was disposed of by repression, but this happened after the genital organization had been reached.

This time we will not lose sight of the part played by anxiety. We have said that as soon as the ego recognizes the danger of castration it gives the signal of anxiety and inhibits through the pleasure-unpleasure agency (in a way which we cannot as yet understand) the impending cathectic process in the id. At the same time the phobia is formed. And now the castration anxiety is directed to a different object and expressed in a distorted form, so that the patient is afraid, not of being castrated by his father, but of being bitten by a horse or devoured by a wolf. This substitutive formation has two obvious advantages. In the first place it avoids a conflict due to ambivalence (for the father was a loved object, too), and in the second place it enables the ego to cease generating anxiety. For the anxiety belonging to a phobia is conditional; it only emerges when the object of it is perceived—and rightly so, since it is only then that the danger-situation is present. There is no need to be afraid of being castrated by a father who is not there. On the other hand one cannot get rid of a father; he can appear whenever he chooses. But if he is replaced by an animal, all one has to do is to avoid the sight of it—that is, its presence—in order to be free from danger and anxiety. 'Little Hans', therefore, imposed a restriction upon his ego. He produced the inhibition of not leaving the house, so as not to come across any horses. The young Russian had an even easier time of it, for it was hardly a privation for him not to look at a particular picture-book any more. If his naughty sister had not kept on showing him the book with the picture of the wolf standing upright in it, he would have been able to feel safe from his fear.[1]

On a previous occasion I have stated that phobias have the character of a projection in that they replace an internal, instinctual danger by an external, perceptual one. The advantage of this is that the subject can protect himself against an external danger by fleeing from it and avoiding the perception of it, whereas it is useless to flee from dangers that arise from within.[2] This statement of mine was not incorrect, but it did not go below the surface of things. For an instinctual demand is, after all, not dangerous in itself; it only becomes so inasmuch as it entails a real external danger, the danger of castration. Thus what happens in a phobia in the last resort is merely that one external danger is replaced by another. The view that in a phobia the ego is able to escape anxiety by means of avoidance or of inhibitory symptoms fits in very well with the theory that that anxiety is only an affective signal and that no alteration has taken place in the economic situation.

The anxiety felt in animal phobias is, therefore, an affective reaction on the part of the ego to danger; and the danger which is being signalled in this way is the danger of castration. This anxiety differs in no respect from the realistic anxiety which the ego normally feels in situations of danger, except that its content remains unconscious and only becomes conscious in the form of a distortion.

The same will prove true, I think, of the phobias of adults, although the material which their neuroses work over is much more abundant and there are some additional factors in the formation of the symptoms. Fundamentally the position is identical. The agoraphobic patient imposes a restric-

---

[1][*Standard Ed.*, **17**, 15–16.]
[2][See the account of phobias given in Section IV of Freud's metapsychological paper on 'The Unconscious' (1915*e*), *Standard Ed.*, **14**, 182–4. See also Editor's Introduction, p. xxix above.]

tion on his ego so as to escape a certain instinctual danger—namely, the danger of giving way to his erotic desires. For if he did so the danger of being castrated, or some similar danger, would once more be conjured up as it was in his childhood. I may cite as an instance the case of a young man who became agoraphobic because he was afraid of yielding to the solicitations of prostitutes and of contracting a syphilitic infection from them as a punishment.

I am well aware that a number of cases exhibit a more complicated structure and that many other repressed instinctual impulses can enter into a phobia. But they are only tributary streams which have for the most part joined the main current of the neurosis at a later stage. The symptomatology of agoraphobia is complicated by the fact that the ego does not confine itself to making a renunciation. In order to rob the situation of danger it does more: it usually effects a temporal regression[3] to infancy (in extreme cases, to a time when the subject was in his mother's womb and protected against the dangers which threaten him in the present). Such a regression now becomes a condition whose fulfilment exempts the ego from making its renunciation. For instance, an agoraphobic patient may be able to walk in the street provided he is accompanied, like a small child, by someone he knows and trusts; or, for the same reason, he may be able to go out alone provided he remains within a certain distance of his own house and does not go to places which are not familiar to him or where people do not know him. What these stipulations are will depend in each case on the infantile factors which dominate him through his neurosis. The phobia of being alone is unambiguous in its meaning, irre-

---

[3][The term 'temporal regression' is used by Freud very rarely. It appears at the beginning of the fifth of his Clark University lectures (1910*a*), *Standard Ed.*, 11, 49, in a paragraph added in 1914 to *The Interpretation of Dreams* (1900*a*), *Standard Ed.*, 5, 548, and in a passage in the metapsychological paper on dreams (1917*d*), *Standard Ed.*, 14, 222–3.]

spective of any infantile regression: it is, ultimately, an endeavour to avoid the temptation to indulge in solitary masturbation. Infantile regression can, of course, only take place
when the subject is no longer a child.

A phobia generally sets in after a first anxiety attack has
been experienced in specific circumstances, such as in the
street or in a train or in solitude. Thereafter the anxiety is
held in ban by the phobia, but it re-emerges whenever the
protective condition cannot be fulfilled. The mechanism of
phobia does good service as a means of defence and tends
to be very stable. A continuation of the defensive struggle,
in the shape of a struggle against the symptom, occurs frequently but not invariably.

What we have learnt about anxiety in phobias is applica-
ble to obsessional neuroses as well. In this respect it is not
difficult for us to put obsessional neuroses on all fours with
phobias. In the former, the mainspring of all later symptom-
formation is clearly the ego's fear of its super-ego. The
danger-situation from which the ego must get away is the
hostility of the super-ego. There is no trace of projection
here; the danger is completely internalized. But if we ask
ourselves what it is that the ego fears from the super-ego, we
cannot but think that the punishment threatened by the
latter must be an extension of the punishment of castration.
Just as the father has become depersonalized in the shape
of the super-ego, so has the fear of castration at his hands
become transformed into an undefined social or moral anxiety.[4] But this anxiety is concealed. The ego escapes it by

---

[4] [*'Gewissensangst'*, literally 'conscience anxiety'. This word is a cause of
constant trouble to the translator. In ordinary usage it means no more than
'qualms of conscience'. But often in Freud, as in the present passage, stress
is laid on the factor of anxiety in the concept. Sometimes, even, it might
be rendered 'fear of conscience' where the distinction between 'conscience'
and 'super-ego' is not sharply drawn. The fullest discussion of these questions will be found in Chapters VII and VIII of *Civilization and its
Discontents* (1930a).]

obediently carrying out the commands, precautions and penances that have been enjoined on it. If it is impeded in doing so, it is at once overtaken by an extremely distressing feeling of discomfort which may be regarded as an equivalent of anxiety and which the patients themselves liken to anxiety.

The conclusion we have come to, then, is this. Anxiety is a reaction to a situation of danger. It is obviated by the ego's doing something to avoid that situation or to withdraw from it. It might be said that symptoms are created so as to avoid the generating of anxiety. But this does not go deep enough. It would be truer to say that symptoms are created so as to avoid a *danger-situation* whose presence has been signalled by the generation of anxiety. In the cases that we have discussed, the danger concerned was the danger of castration or of something traceable back to castration.

If anxiety is a reaction of the ego to danger, we shall be tempted to regard the traumatic neuroses, which so often follow upon a narrow escape from death, as a direct result of a fear of death (or fear *for* life) and to dismiss from our minds the question of castration and the dependent relationships of the ego [p. 15]. Most of those who observed the traumatic neuroses that occurred during the last war[5] took this line, and triumphantly announced that proof was now forthcoming that a threat to the instinct of self-preservation could by itself produce a neurosis without any admixture of sexual factors and without requiring any of the complicated hypotheses of psycho-analysis. It is in fact greatly to be regretted that not a single analysis of a traumatic neurosis of any value is extant.[6] And it is to be regretted, not because such an analysis would contradict the aetiological importance of sexuality—for any such contradiction has long since

---

[5] [The first World War.]
[6] [See Freud's discussion of the war neuroses (1919*d*).]

been disposed of by the introduction of the concept of narcissism, which brings the libidinal cathexis of the ego into line with the cathexes of objects and emphasizes the libidinal character of the instinct of self-preservation—but because, in the absence of any analyses of this kind, we have lost a most precious opportunity of drawing decisive conclusions about the relations between anxiety and the formation of symptoms. In view of all that we know about the structure of the comparatively simple neuroses of everyday life, it would seem highly improbable that a neurosis could come into being merely because of the objective presence of danger, without any participation of the deeper levels of the mental apparatus. But the unconscious seems to contain nothing that could give any content to our concept of the annihilation of life. Castration can be pictured on the basis of the daily experience of the faeces being separated from the body or on the basis of losing the mother's breast at weaning.[7] But nothing resembling death can ever have been experienced; or if it has, as in fainting, it has left no observable traces behind. I am therefore inclined to adhere to the view that the fear of death should be regarded as analogous to the fear of castration and that the situation to which the ego is reacting is one of being abandoned by the protecting super-ego—the powers of destiny—so that it has no longer any safeguard against all the dangers that surround it.[8] In addition, it must be remembered that in the experiences which lead to a traumatic neurosis the protective shield against external stimuli is broken through and excessive amounts of excitation impinge upon the mental apparatus [cf. p. 13]; so that we have here a second possibility—that

---

[7][See a footnote added in 1923 to the 'Little Hans' case history, *Standard Ed.*, 10, 8–9.]

[8][Cf. the last few paragraphs of *The Ego and the Id* (1923*b*), and below, p. 71.]

anxiety is not only being signalled as an affect but is also being freshly created out of the economic conditions of the situation.

The statement I have just made, to the effect that the ego has been prepared to expect castration by having undergone constantly repeated object-losses, places the question of anxiety in a new light. We have hitherto regarded it as an affective signal of danger; but now, since the danger is so often one of castration, it appears to us as a reaction to a loss, a separation. Even though a number of considerations immediately arise which make against this view, we cannot but be struck by one very remarkable correlation. The first experience of anxiety which an individual goes through (in the case of human beings, at all events) is birth, and, objectively speaking, birth is a separation from the mother. It could be compared to a castration of the mother (by equating the child with a penis). Now it would be very satisfactory if anxiety, as a symbol of a separation, were to be repeated on every subsequent occasion on which a separation took place. But unfortunately we are prevented from making use of this correlation by the fact that birth is not experienced subjectively as a separation from the mother, since the foetus, being a completely narcissistic creature, is totally unaware of her existence as an object. Another adverse argument is that we know what the affective reactions to a separation are: they are pain and mourning, not anxiety. Incidentally, it may be remembered that in discussing the question of mourning we also failed to discover why it should be such a painful thing.[9]

---

[9][See 'Mourning and Melancholia' (1917*e*), *Standard Ed.*, 14, 244–5. Freud returns to this subject in Addendum C, p. 106 ff. below.]

VIII

The time has come to pause and consider. What we clearly want is to find something that will tell us what anxiety really is, some criterion that will enable us to distinguish true statements about it from false ones. But this is not easy to get. Anxiety is not so simple a matter. Up till now we have arrived at nothing but contradictory views about it, none of which can, to the unprejudiced eye, be given preference over the others. I therefore propose to adopt a different procedure. I propose to assemble, quite impartially, all the facts that we know about anxiety without expecting to arrive at a fresh synthesis.

Anxiety, then, is in the first place something that is felt. We call it an affective state, although we are also ignorant of what an affect is. As a feeling, anxiety has a very marked character of unpleasure. But that is not the whole of its quality. Not every unpleasure can be called anxiety, for there are other feelings, such as tension, pain or mourning, which have the character of unpleasure. Thus anxiety must have other distinctive features besides this quality of unpleasure. Can we succeed in understanding the differences between these various unpleasurable affects?

We can at any rate note one or two things about the feeling of anxiety. Its unpleasurable character seems to have a note of its own—something not very obvious, whose presence is difficult to prove yet which is in all likelihood there. But besides having this special feature which is difficult to isolate, we notice that anxiety is accompanied by fairly definite physical sensations which can be referred to particular organs of the body. As we are not concerned here with the physiology of anxiety, we shall content ourselves with mentioning a few representatives of these sensations. The clearest and most frequent ones are those connected with the respiratory organs and with the heart.[1] They provide evidence that motor innervations—that is, processes of discharge—play a part in the general phenomenon of anxiety.

Analysis of anxiety-states therefore reveals the existence of (1) a specific character of unpleasure, (2) acts of discharge and (3) perceptions of those acts. The two last points indicate at once a difference between states of anxiety and other similar states, like those of mourning and pain. The latter do not have any motor manifestation; or if they have, the manifestation is not an integral part of the whole state but is distinct from it as being a result of it or a reaction to it. Anxiety, then, is a special state of unpleasure with acts of discharge along particular paths. In accordance with our general views[2] we should be inclined to think that anxiety is based upon an increase of excitation which on the one hand produces the character of unpleasure and on the other finds relief through the acts of discharge already mentioned. But a purely physiological account of this sort will scarcely satisfy us. We are tempted to assume the presence of a historical factor which binds the sensations of anxiety and its innervations firmly together. We assume, in other words,

---

[1] [Cf. paragraph 3 of Section I of Freud's first paper on anxiety neurosis (1895*b*).]

[2] [As expressed, for instance, in the opening pages of *Beyond the Pleasure Principle* (1920g), *Standard Ed.*, 18, 7 ff.]

that an anxiety-state is the reproduction of some experience which contained the necessary conditions for such an increase of excitation and a discharge along particular paths, and that from this circumstance the unpleasure of anxiety receives its specific character. In man, birth provides a prototypic experience of this kind, and we are therefore inclined to regard anxiety-states as a reproduction of the trauma of birth. [See above, p. 12 f.]

This does not imply that anxiety occupies an exceptional position among the affective states. In my opinion the other affects are also reproductions of very early, perhaps even pre-individual, experiences of vital importance; and I should be inclined to regard them as universal, typical and innate hysterical attacks, as compared to the recently and individually acquired attacks which occur in hysterical neuroses and whose origin and significance as mnemic symbols have been revealed by analysis. It would be very desirable, of course, to be able to demonstrate the truth of this view in a number of such affects—a thing which is still very far from being the case.[3]

The view that anxiety goes back to the event of birth raises immediate objections which have to be met. It may be argued that anxiety is a reaction which, in all probability, is common to every organism, certainly every organism of a higher order, whereas birth is only experienced by the mammals; and it is doubtful whether in all of them, even, birth has the significance of a trauma. Therefore there can be anxiety without the prototype of birth. But this objection takes us beyond the barrier that divides psychology from biology. It may be that, precisely because anxiety has an

---

[3][This notion is probably derived from Darwin's *Expression of the Emotions* (1872), which was quoted by Freud in a similar connection in *Studies on Hysteria* (1895*d*), *Standard Ed.*, 2, 181. See Editor's Introduction, p. xxxiv.]

indispensable biological function to fulfil as a reaction to a state of danger, it is differently contrived in different organisms. We do not know, besides, whether anxiety involves the same sensations and innervations in organisms far removed from man as it does in man himself. Thus there is no good argument here against the view that, in man, anxiety is modelled upon the process of birth.

If the structure and origin of anxiety are as described, the next question is: what is the function of anxiety and on what occasions is it reproduced? The answer seems to be obvious and convincing: anxiety arose originally as a reaction to a state of *danger* and it is reproduced whenever a state of that kind recurs.

This answer, however, raises further considerations. The innervations involved in the original state of anxiety probably had a meaning and purpose, in just the same way as the muscular movements which accompany a first hysterical attack. In order to understand a hysterical attack, all one has to do is to look for the situation in which the movements in question formed part of an appropriate and expedient action. Thus at birth it is probable that the innervation, in being directed to the respiratory organs, is preparing the way for the activity of the lungs, and, in accelerating the heart-beat, is helping to keep the blood free from toxic substances. Naturally, when the anxiety-state is reproduced later as an affect it will be lacking in any such expediency, just as are the repetitions of a hysterical attack. When the individual is placed in a new situation of danger it may well be quite inexpedient for him to respond with an anxiety-state (which is a reaction to an earlier danger) instead of initiating a reaction appropriate to the current danger. But his behavior may become expedient once more if the danger-situation is recognized as it approaches and is signalled by an outbreak of anxiety. In that case he can at once get rid of his anxiety by having recourse to more suitable measures. Thus we see that there are two ways in which anxiety can emerge: in an inexpedient way, when a new situation of danger has occurred, or in an expedient way in order to give a signal and prevent such a situation from occurring.

But what is a 'danger'? In the act of birth there is a real danger to life. We know what this means objectively; but in a psychological sense it says nothing at all to us. The danger of birth has as yet no psychical content. We cannot possibly suppose that the foetus has any sort of knowledge that there is a possibility of its life being destroyed. It can only be aware of some vast disturbance in the economy of its narcissistic libido. Large sums of excitation crowd in upon it, giving rise to new kinds of feelings of unpleasure, and some organs acquire an increased cathexis, thus foreshadowing the object-cathexis which will soon set in. What elements in all this will be made use of as the sign of a 'danger-situation'?

Unfortunately far too little is known about the mental make-up of a new-born baby to make a direct answer possible. I cannot even vouch for the validity of the description I have just given. It is easy to say that the baby will repeat its affect of anxiety in every situation which recalls the event of birth. The important thing to know is what recalls the event and what it is that is recalled.

All we can do is to examine the occasions on which infants in arms or somewhat older children show readiness to produce anxiety. In his book on the trauma of birth, Rank (1924) has made a determined attempt to establish a relationship between the earliest phobias of children and the impressions made on them by the event of birth. But I do not think he has been successful. His theory is open to two objections. In the first place, he assumes that the infant has received certain sensory impressions, in particular of a visual kind, at the time of birth, the renewal of which can recall to its memory the trauma of birth and thus evoke a reaction of anxiety. This assumption is quite unfounded and extremely improbable. It is not credible that a child should retain any but tactile and general sensations relating to the process of birth. If, later on, children show fear of small animals that disappear into holes or emerge from them, this reaction, according to Rank, is due to their perceiving an analogy. But it is an analogy of which they cannot be aware. In the second place, in considering these later anxiety-situations Rank dwells, as suits him best, now on the child's recollection of its happy intra-uterine existence, now on its recollection of the traumatic disturbance which interrupted that existence—which leaves the door wide open for arbitrary interpretation. There are, moreover, certain examples of childhood anxiety which directly traverse his theory. When, for instance, a child is left alone in the dark one would expect it, according to his view, to welcome the re-establishment of the intra-uterine situation; yet it is precisely on such occasions that the child reacts with anxiety. And if this is explained by saying that the child is being reminded of the interruption which the event of birth made in its intra-uterine happiness, it becomes impossible to shut one's eyes any longer to the far-fetched character of such explanations.[4]

I am driven to the conclusion that the earliest phobias of infancy cannot be directly traced back to impressions of the act of birth and that so far they have not been explained. A certain preparedness for anxiety is undoubtedly present in the infant in arms. But this preparedness for anxiety, instead of being at its maximum immediately after birth and then slowly decreasing, does not emerge till later, as mental development proceeds, and lasts over a certain period of child-

---

[4] [Rank's theory is further discussed below, p. 83 ff.]

hood. If these early phobias persist beyond that period one is inclined to suspect the presence of a neurotic disturbance, although it is not at all clear what their relation is to the undoubted neuroses that appear later on in childhood.

Only a few of the manifestations of anxiety in children are comprehensible to us, and we must confine our attention to them. They occur, for instance, when a child is alone, or in the dark,[5] or when it finds itself with an unknown person instead of one to whom it is used—such as its mother. These three instances can be reduced to a single condition— namely, that of missing someone who is loved and longed for. But here, I think, we have the key to an understanding of anxiety and to a reconciliation of the contradictions that seem to beset it.

The child's mnemic image of the person longed for is no doubt intensely cathected, probably in a hallucinatory way at first. But this has no effect; and now it seems as though the longing turns into anxiety. This anxiety has all the appearance of being an expression of the child's feeling at its wits' end, as though in its still very undeveloped state it did not know how better to cope with its cathexis of longing. Here anxiety appears as a reaction to the felt loss of the object; and we are at once reminded of the fact that castration anxiety, too, is a fear of being separated from a highly valued object, and that the earliest anxiety of all—the 'primal anxiety' of birth—is brought about on the occasion of a separation from the mother.

But a moment's reflection takes us beyond this question of loss of object. The reason why the infant in arms wants to perceive the presence of its mother is only because it already knows by experience that she satisfies all its needs

---

[5][Cf. a footnote to Section 5 of the third of Freud's *Three Essays* (1905d), *Standard Ed.*, 7, 224.]

without delay. The situation, then, which it regards as a 'danger' and against which it wants to be safeguarded is that of non-satisfaction, of a *growing tension due to need,* against which it is helpless. I think that if we adopt this view all the facts fall into place. The situation of non-satisfaction in which the amounts of stimulation rise to an unpleasurable height without its being possible for them to be mastered psychically or discharged must for the infant be analogous to the experience of being born—must be a repetition of the situation of danger. What both situations have in common is the economic disturbance caused by an accumulation of amounts of stimulation which require to be disposed of. It is this factor, then, which is the real essence of the 'danger'. In both cases the reaction of anxiety sets in. (This reaction is still an expedient one in the infant in arms, for the discharge, being directed into the respiratory and vocal muscular apparatus, now calls its mother to it, just as it activated the lungs of the new-born baby to get rid of the internal stimuli.) It is unnecessary to suppose that the child carries anything more with it from the time of its birth than this way of indicating the presence of danger.

When the infant has found out by experience that an external, perceptible object can put an end to the dangerous situation which is reminiscent of birth, the content of the danger it fears is displaced from the economic situation on to the condition which determined that situation, viz., the loss of object. It is the absence of the mother that is now the danger; and as soon as that danger arises the infant gives the signal of anxiety, before the dreaded economic situation has set in. This change constitutes a first great step forward in the provision made by the infant for its self-preservation, and at the same time represents a transition from the automatic and involuntary fresh appearance of anxiety to the intentional reproduction of anxiety as a signal of danger.

In these two aspects, as an automatic phenomenon and as a rescuing signal, anxiety is seen to be a product of the infant's mental helplessness which is a natural counterpart of its biological helplessness. The striking coincidence by which the anxiety of the new-born baby and the anxiety of the infant in arms are both conditioned by separation from the mother does not need to be explained on psychological lines. It can be accounted for simply enough biologically; for, just as the mother originally satisfied all the needs of the foetus through the apparatus of her own body, so now, after its birth, she continues to do so, though partly by other means. There is much more continuity between intra-uterine life and earliest infancy than the impressive caesura[6] of the act of birth would have us believe. What happens is that the child's biological situation as a foetus is replaced for it by a psychical object-relation to its mother. But we must not forget that during its intra-uterine life the mother was not an object for the foetus, and that at that time there were no objects at all. It is obvious that in this scheme of things there is no place for the abreaction of the birth-trauma. We cannot find that anxiety has any function other than that of being a signal for the avoidance of a danger-situation.

The significance of the loss of object as a determinant of anxiety extends considerably further. For the next transformation of anxiety, viz. the castration anxiety belonging to the phallic phase, is also a fear of separation and is thus attached to the same determinant. In this case the danger is of being separated from one's genitals. Ferenczi [1925] has traced, quite correctly, I think, a clear line of connection between this fear and the fears contained in the earlier

---

6[*'Caesur.'* In the 1926 German edition only, this was misprinted *'Censur* (censorship)'. The word 'caesura' is a term derived from classical prosody, and means a particular kind of break in a line of verse.]

situations of danger. The high degree of narcissistic value which the penis possesses can appeal to the fact that that organ is a guarantee to its owner that he can be once more united to his mother—i.e. to a substitute for her—in the act of copulation. Being deprived of it amounts to a renewed separation from her, and this in its turn means being help-lessly exposed to an unpleasurable tension due to instinctual need, as was the case at birth. But the need whose increase is feared is now a specific one belonging to the genital libido and is no longer an indeterminate one, as it was in the period of infancy. It may be added that for a man who is impotent (that is, who is inhibited by the threat of castration) the substitute for copulation is a phantasy of returning into his mother's womb. Following Ferenczi's line of thought, we might say that the man in question, having tried to bring about his return into his mother's womb by using his genital organ to represent him, is now [in this phantasy] replacing that organ regressively by his whole person.[7]

The progress which the child makes in its development—its growing independence, the sharper division of its mental apparatus into several agencies, the advent of new needs—cannot fail to exert an influence upon the content of the danger-situation. We have already traced the change of that content from loss of the mother as an object to castration. The next change is caused by the power of the super-ego. With the depersonalization of the parental agency from which castration was feared, the danger becomes less de-fined. Castration anxiety develops into moral anxiety—so-cial anxiety—and it is not so easy now to know what the anxiety is about. The formula, 'separation and expulsion from the horde', only applies to that later portion of the

---

[7][Freud had already discussed this phantasy in the 'Wolf Man' analysis (1918*b*), *Standard Ed.*, 17, 100 2.]

super-ego which has been formed on the basis of social prototypes, not to the nucleus of the super-ego, which corresponds to the introjected parental agency. Putting it more generally, what the ego regards as the danger and responds to with an anxiety-signal is that the super-ego should be angry with it or punish it or cease to love it. The final transformation which the fear of the super-ego undergoes is, it seems to me, the fear of death (or fear for life) which is a fear of the super-ego projected on to the powers of destiny.[8]

At one time I attached some importance to the view that what was used as a discharge of anxiety was the cathexis which had been withdrawn in the process of repression.[9] To-day this seems to me of scarcely any interest. The reason for this is that whereas I formerly believed that anxiety invariably arose automatically by an economic process, my present conception of anxiety as a signal given by the ego in order to affect the pleasure-unpleasure agency does away with the necessity of considering the economic factor. Of course there is nothing to be said against the idea that it is precisely the energy that has been liberated by being withdrawn through repression which is used by the ego to arouse the affect; but it is no longer of any importance which portion of energy is employed for this purpose. [Cf. Editor's Introduction, p. xxix.]

This new view of things calls for an examination of another assertion of mine—namely, that the ego is the actual seat of anxiety.[10] I think this proposition still holds good. There is no reason to assign any manifestation of anxiety to the super-ego; while the expression 'anxiety of the id' would

---

[8][Cf. above, p. 58.]

[9][See, for instance, Section IV of Freud's metapsychological paper on 'The Unconscious' (1915e), *Standard Ed.*, 14, 182.]

[10][This will be found a couple of pages before the end of *The Ego and the Id* (1923b).]

stand in need of correction, though rather as to its form than its substance. Anxiety is an affective state and as such can, of course, only be felt by the ego. The id cannot have anxiety as the ego can; for it is not an organization and cannot make a judgement about situations of danger. On the other hand it very often happens that processes take place or begin to take place in the id which cause the ego to produce anxiety. Indeed, it is probable that the earliest repressions as well as most of the later ones are motivated by an ego-anxiety of this sort in regard to particular processes in the id. Here again we are rightly distinguishing between two cases: the case in which something occurs in the id which activates one of the danger-situations for the ego and induces the latter to give the anxiety-signal for inhibition to take place, and the case in which a situation analogous to the trauma of birth is established in the id and an automatic reaction of anxiety ensues. The two cases may be brought closer together if it is pointed out that the second case corresponds to the earliest and original danger-situation, while the first case corresponds to any one of the later determinants of anxiety that have been derived from it; or, as applied to the disorders which we in fact come across, that the second case is operative in the aetiology of the 'actual' neuroses, while the first remains typical for that of the psychoneuroses.

We see, then, that it is not so much a question of taking back our earlier findings as of bringing them into line with more recent discoveries. It is still an undeniable fact that in sexual abstinence, in improper interference with the course of sexual excitation or if the latter is diverted from being worked over psychically,[11] anxiety arises directly out of libido; in other words, that the ego is reduced to a state of

---

[11][*'Psychische Verarbeitung'*, literally, 'psychical working-over'. The phrase will be found in Section III of Freud's first paper on anxiety neurosis (1895*b*), of which the whole of the present passage is an echo.]

helplessness in the face of an excessive tension due to need, as it was in the situation of birth, and that anxiety is then generated. Here once more, though the matter is of little importance, it is very possible that what finds discharge in the generating of anxiety is precisely the surplus of unutilized libido.[12] As we know, a psychoneurosis is especially liable to develop on the basis of an 'actual' neurosis. This looks as though the ego were attempting to save itself from anxiety, which it has learned to keep in suspension for a while, and to bind it by the formation of symptoms. Analysis of the traumatic war neuroses—a term which, incidentally, covers a great variety of disorders—would probably have shown that a number of them possess some characteristics of the 'actual' neuroses. [Cf. above, p. 57.]

In describing the evolution of the various danger-situations from their prototype, the act of birth, I have had no intention of asserting that every later determinant of anxiety completely invalidates the preceding one. It is true that, as the development of the ego goes on, the earlier danger-situations tend to lose their force and to be set aside, so that we might say that each period of the individual's life has its appropriate determinant of anxiety. Thus the danger of psychical helplessness is appropriate to the period of life when his ego is immature; the danger of loss of object, to early childhood when he is still dependent on others; the danger of castration, to the phallic phase; and the fear of his super-ego, to the latency period. Nevertheless, all these danger-situations and determinants of anxiety can persist side by side and cause the ego to react to them with anxiety at a period later than the appropriate one; or, again, several of them can come into operation at the same time. It is possible, moreover, that there is a fairly close relationship be-

---

[12][Cf. the similar remark at the end of the last paragraph but one, but see also the Editor's Introduction, p. xxviii above.]

tween the danger-situation that is operative and the form taken by the ensuing neurosis.[13]

When, in an earlier part of this discussion, we found that the danger of castration was of importance in more than one neurotic illness, we put ourselves on guard against overestimating that factor, since it could not be a decisive one for the female sex, who are undoubtedly more subject to neuroses than men. [See p. 50.] We now see that there is no danger of our regarding castration anxiety as the sole motive force of the defensive processes which lead to neurosis. I have shown elsewhere[14] how little girls, in the course of

---

[13]Since the differentiation of the ego and the id, our interest in the problems of repression, too, was bound to receive a fresh impetus. Up till then we had been content to confine our interest to those aspects of repression which concerned the ego—the keeping away from consciousness and from motility, and the formation of substitutes (symptoms). With regard to the repressed instinctual impulses themselves, we assumed that they remained unaltered in the unconscious for an indefinite length of time. But now our interest is turned to the vicissitudes of the repressed and we begin to suspect that it is not self-evident, perhaps not even usual, that those impulses should remain unaltered and unalterable in this way. There is no doubt that the original impulses have been inhibited and deflected from their aim through repression. But has the portion of them in the unconscious maintained itself and been proof against the influences of life that tend to alter and depreciate them? In other words, do the old wishes, about whose former existence analysis tells us, still exist? The answer seems ready to hand and certain. It is that the old, repressed wishes must still be present in the unconscious since we still find their derivatives, the symptoms, in operation. But this answer is not sufficient. It does not enable us to decide between two possibilities: either that the old wish is now operating only through its derivatives, having transferred the whole of its cathectic energy to them, or that it is itself still in existence too. If its fate has been to exhaust itself in cathecting its derivatives, there is yet a third possibility. In the course of the neurosis it may have become re-animated by regression, anachronistic though it may now be. These are no idle speculations. There are many things about mental life, both normal and pathological, which seem to call for the raising of such questions. In my paper, 'The Dissolution of the Oedipus Complex' (1924*d*), I had occasion to notice the difference between the mere repression and the real removal of an old wishful impulse.
[14][See the second half of the paper on the consequences of the anatomical distinction between the sexes (1925*j*).]

their development, are led into making a tender object-cathexis by their castration complex. It is precisely in women that the danger-situation of loss of object seems to have remained the most effective. All we need to do is to make a slight modification in our description of their determinant of anxiety, in the sense that it is no longer a matter of feeling the want of, or actually losing the object itself, but of losing the object's love. Since there is no doubt that hysteria has a strong affinity with femininity, just as obsessional neurosis has with masculinity, it appears probable that, as a determinant of anxiety, loss of love plays much the same part in hysteria as the threat of castration does in phobias and fear of the super-ego in obsessional neurosis.

IX

What is now left for us is to consider the relationship between the formation of symptoms and the generating of anxiety.

There seem to be two very widely held opinions on this subject. One is that anxiety is itself a symptom of neurosis. The other is that there is a much more intimate relation between the two. According to the second opinion, symptoms are only formed in order to avoid anxiety: they bind the psychical energy which would otherwise be discharged as anxiety. Thus anxiety would be the fundamental phenomenon and main problem of neurosis.

That this latter opinion is at least in part true is shown by some striking examples. If an agoraphobic patient who has been accompanied into the street is left alone there, he will produce an anxiety attack. Or if an obsessional neurotic is prevented from washing his hands after having touched something, he will become a prey to almost unbearable anxiety. It is plain, then, that the purpose and the result of the imposed condition of being accompanied in the street and the obsessional act of washing the hands were to obviate outbreaks of anxiety of this kind. In this sense every inhibition which the ego imposes on itself can be called a symptom.

Since we have traced back the generating of anxiety to a situation of danger, we shall prefer to say that symptoms are created in order to remove the ego from a situation of danger. If the symptoms are prevented from being formed, the danger does in fact materialize; that is, a situation analogous to birth is established in which the ego is helpless in the face of a constantly increasing instinctual demand—the earliest and original determinant of anxiety. Thus in our view the relation between anxiety and symptom is less close than was supposed, for we have inserted the factor of the danger-situation between them. We can also add that the generating of anxiety sets symptom formation going and is, indeed, a necessary prerequisite of it. For if the ego did not arouse the pleasure-unpleasure agency by generating anxiety, it would not obtain the power to arrest the process which is preparing in the id and which threatens[1] danger. There is in all this an evident inclination to limit to a minimum the amount of anxiety generated and to employ it only as a signal; for to do otherwise would only result in feeling in another place the unpleasure which the instinctual process was threatening to produce, and that would not be a success from the standpoint of the pleasure principle, although it is one that occurs often enough in the neuroses.

Symptom-formation, then, does in fact put an end to the danger-situation. It has two aspects: one, hidden from view, brings about the alteration in the id in virtue of which the ego is removed from danger; the other, presented openly, shows what has been created in place of the instinctual process that has been affected—namely, the substitutive formation.

It would, however, be more correct to ascribe to the *defensive process* what we have just said about symptom-

---

[1] [I.e. between anxiety and neurosis.]

formation and to use the latter term as synonomous with substitute-formation. It will then be clear that the defensive process is analogous to the flight by means of which the ego removes itself from a danger that threatens it from outside. The defensive process is an attempt at flight from an instinctual danger. An examination of the weak points in this comparison will make things clearer.

One objection to it is that loss of an object (or loss of love on the part of the object) and the threat of castration are just as much dangers coming from outside as, let us say, a ferocious animal would be; they are not instinctual dangers. Nevertheless, the two cases are not the same. A wolf would probably attack us irrespectively of our behavior towards it; but the loved person would not cease to love us nor should we be threatened with castration if we did not entertain certain feelings and intentions within us. Thus such instinctual impulses are determinants of external dangers and so become dangerous in themselves; and we can now proceed against the external danger by taking measures against the internal ones. In phobias of animals the danger seems to be still felt entirely as an external one, just as it has undergone an external displacement in the symptom. In obsessional neuroses the danger is much more internalized. That portion of anxiety in regard to the super-ego which constitutes *social* anxiety still represents an internal substitute for an external danger, while the other portion—*moral* anxiety—is already completely endopsychic.[2]

Another objection is that in an attempt at flight from an impending external danger all that the subject is doing is to increase the distance between himself and what is threaten-

---

[2][Much of the present discussion is a re-assessment of the arguments which Freud had used in his metapsychological papers on 'Repression' (1915*d*) and 'The Unconscious' (1915*e*). See, in particular, *Standard Ed.*, 14, 153–5, and 181–4.—For 'moral anxiety' cf. footnote, p. 56.]

ing him. He is not preparing to defend himself against it or attempting to alter anything about it, as would be the case if he attacked the wolf with a stick or shot at it with a gun. But the defensive process seems to do something more than would correspond to an attempt at flight. It joins issue with the threatening instinctual process and somehow suppresses it or deflects it from its aims and thus renders it innocuous. This objection seems unimpeachable and must be given due weight. I think it is probable that there are some defensive processes which can truly be likened to an attempt at flight, while in others the ego takes a much more active line of self-protection and initiates vigorous counter-measures. But perhaps the whole analogy between defence and flight is invalidated by the fact that both the ego and the instinct in the id are parts of the same organization, not separate entities like the wolf and the child, so that any kind of behaviour on the part of the ego will result in an alteration in the instinctual process as well.

This study of the determinants of anxiety has, as it were, shown the defensive behaviour of the ego transfigured in a rational light. Each situation of danger corresponds to a particular period of life or a particular developmental phase of the mental apparatus and appears to be justifiable for it. In early infancy the individual is really not equipped to master psychically the large sums of excitation that reach him whether from without or from within. Again, at a certain period of life his most important interest really is that the people he is dependent on should not withdraw their loving care of him. Later on in his boyhood, when he feels that his father is a powerful rival in regard to his mother and becomes aware of his own aggressive inclinations towards him and of his sexual intentions towards his mother, he really is justified in being afraid of his father; and his fear of being punished by him can find expression through phylogenetic reinforcement in the fear of being castrated. Finally, as he enters into social relationships, it really is necessary for him to be afraid of his super-ego, to have a conscience; and the absence of that factor would give rise to severe conflicts, dangers and so on.

But this last point raises a fresh problem. Instead of the affect of anxiety let us take, for a moment, another affect—that of pain, for instance. It seems quite normal that at four years of age a girl should weep painfully if her doll is broken; or at six, if her governess reproves her; or at sixteen, if she is slighted by her young man; or at twenty-five, perhaps, if a child of her own dies. Each of these determinants of pain has its own time and each passes away when that time is over. Only the final and definitive determinants remain throughout life. We should think it strange if this same girl, after she had grown to be a wife and mother, were to cry over some worthless trinket that had been damaged. Yet that is how the neurotic behaves. Although all the agencies for mastering stimuli have long ago been developed within wide limits in his mental apparatus, and although he is sufficiently grown-up to satisfy most of his needs for himself and has long ago learnt that castration is no longer practised as a punishment, he nevertheless behaves as though the old danger-situations still existed, and keeps hold of all the earlier determinants of anxiety.

Why this should be so calls for a rather long reply. First of all, we must sift the facts. In a great number of cases the old determinants of anxiety do really lapse, after having produced neurotic reactions. The phobias of very young children, fears of being alone or in the dark or with strangers—phobias which can almost be called normal—usually pass off later on; the child 'grows out of them', as we say about some other disturbances of childhood. Animal phobias, which are of such frequent occurrence, undergo the same fate and many conversion hysterias of early years find no continuation in later life. Ceremonial actions appear extremely often in the latency period, but only a very small percentage of them develop later into a full obsessional neurosis. In general, so far as we can tell from our observations of town children belonging to the white races and living according to fairly high cultural standards, the neuroses of childhood are in the nature of regular episodes in a child's development, although too little attention is still being paid to them. Signs of childhood neuroses can be detected in *all* adult neurotics without exception; but by no means all children who show those signs become neurotic in later life. It must be, therefore, that certain determinants of anxiety are relinquished and certain danger-situations lose their significance as the individual becomes more mature. Moreover, some of these danger-situations manage to survive into later times by modifying their determinants of anxiety so as to bring them up to date. Thus, for instance, a man may retain his fear of castration in the guise of a syphilidophobia, after he has come to know that it is no longer customary to castrate people for indulging their sexual lusts, but that, on the other hand, severe diseases may overtake anyone who thus gives way to his instincts. Other determinants of anxiety, such as fear of the super-ego, are destined not to disappear at all but to accompany people throughout their lives. In that case the neurotic will differ from the normal person in that his reactions to the dangers in question will be unduly strong. Finally, being grown-up affords no absolute protection against a return of the original traumatic anxiety-situation. Each individual has in all probability a limit beyond which his mental apparatus fails in its function of mastering the quantities of excitation which require to be disposed of.

These minor rectifications cannot in any way alter the

fact which is here under discussion, that a great many people remain infantile in their behaviour in regard to danger and do not overcome determinants of anxiety which have grown out of date. To deny this would be to deny the existence of neurosis, for it is precisely such people whom we call neurotics. But how is this possible? Why are not all neuroses episodes in the development of the individual which comes to a close when the next phase is reached? Whence comes the element of persistence in these reactions to danger? Why does the affect of anxiety alone seem to enjoy the advantage over all other affects of evoking reactions which are distinguished from the rest in being abnormal and which, through their inexpediency, run counter to the movement of life? In other words, we have once more come unawares upon the riddle which has so often confronted us: whence does neurosis come—what is its ultimate, its own peculiar *raison d'être?* After tens of years of psychoanalytic labours, we are as much in the dark about this problem as we were at the start.

X

Anxiety is the reaction to danger. One cannot, after all, help suspecting that the reason why the affect of anxiety occupies a unique position in the economy of the mind has something to do with the essential nature of danger. Yet dangers are the common lot of humanity; they are the same for everyone. What we need and cannot lay our finger on is some factor which will explain why some people are able to subject the affect of anxiety, in spite of its peculiar quality, to the normal workings of the mind, or which decides who is doomed to come to grief over that task. Two attempts to find a factor of this kind have been made; and it is natural that such efforts should meet with a sympathetic reception, since they promise help to meet a tormenting need. The two attempts in question are mutually complementary; they approach the problem at opposite ends. The first was made by Alfred Adler more than ten years ago.[1] His contention, reduced to its essence, was that the people who came to grief over the task set them by danger were those who were too greatly impeded by some organic inferiority. If it were true that *simplex sigillum veri*,[2] we should welcome such a solu-

---

[1][See, for instance, Adler, 1907.]
[2][I.e., simplicity is the seal of truth.]

tion [*Lösung*] as a deliverance [*Erlösung*]. But on the contrary, our critical studies of the last ten years have effectively demonstrated the total inadequacy of such an explanation—an explanation, moreover, which sets aside the whole wealth of material that has been discovered by psycho-analysis.

The second attempt was made by Otto Rank in 1923 in his book, *The Trauma of Birth*. [See pp. xxxvi and 65 f.] It would be unjust to put his attempt on the same level as Adler's except in this single point which concerns us here, for it remains on psycho-analytic ground and pursues a psycho-analytic line of thought, so that it may be accepted as a legitimate endeavour to solve the problems of analysis. In this matter of the relation of the individual to danger Rank moves away from the question of organic defect in the individual and concentrates on the variable degree of intensity of the danger. The process of birth is the first situation of danger, and the economic upheaval which it produces becomes the prototype of the reaction of anxiety. We have already [p. 66ff.] traced the line of development which connects this first danger-situation and determinant of anxiety with all the later ones, and we have seen that they all retain a common quality in so far as they signify in a certain sense a separation from the mother—at first only in a biological sense, next as a direct loss of object and later as a loss of object incurred indirectly. The discovery of this extensive concatenation is an undoubted merit of Rank's construction. Now the trauma of birth overtakes each individual with a different degree of intensity, and the violence of his anxiety-reaction varies with the strength of the trauma; and it is the initial amount of anxiety generated in him which, according to Rank, decides whether he will ever learn to control it—whether he will become neurotic or normal.

It is not our business to criticize Rank's hypothesis in detail here. We have only to consider whether it helps to solve our particular problem. His formula—that those people become neurotic in whom the trauma of birth was so strong that they have never been able completely to abreact it—is highly disputable from a theoretical point of view. We do not rightly know what is meant by abreacting the trauma. Taken literally, it implies that the more frequently and the more intensely a neurotic person reproduces the affect of anxiety the more closely will he approach to mental health—an untenable conclusion. It was because it did not tally with the facts that I gave up the theory of abreaction which had played such a large part in the cathartic method. To lay so much stress, too, on the variability in the strength of the birth trauma is to leave no room for the legitimate claims of hereditary constitution as an aetiological factor. For this variability is an organic factor which operates in an accidental fashion in relation to the constitution and is itself dependent on many influences which might be called accidental—as, for instance, on timely assistance in child-birth. Rank's theory completely ignores constitutional factors as well as phylogenetic ones. If, however, we were to try to find a place for the constitutional factor by qualifying his statement with the proviso, let us say, that what is really important is the extent to which the individual reacts to the variable intensity of the trauma of birth, we should be depriving his theory of its significance and should be relegating the new factor introduced by him to a position of minor importance: the factor which decided whether a neurosis should supervene or not would lie in a different, and once more in an unknown, field.

Moreover, the fact that while man shares the process of birth with the other mammals he alone has the privilege over them of possessing a special disposition to neurosis is hardly favourable to Rank's theory. But the main objection to it is that it floats in the air instead of being based upon ascertained observations. No body of evidence has been collected to show that difficult and protracted birth does in fact coincide with the development of a neurosis, or even that children so born exhibit the phenomena of early infantile apprehensiveness more strongly and over a longer period than other children. It might be rejoined that induced labour and births that are easy for the mother may possibly involve a severe trauma for the child. But we can still point out that births which lead to asphyxia would be bound to give clear evidence of the results which are supposed to follow. It should be one of the advantages of Rank's aetiological theory that it postulates a factor whose existence can be verified by observation. And so long as no such attempt at verification has been made it is impossible to assess the theory's value.

On the other hand I cannot identify myself with the view that Rank's theory contradicts the aetiological importance of the sexual instincts as hitherto recognized by psychoanalysis. For his theory only has reference to the individual's relation to the danger-situation, so that it leaves it perfectly open to us to assume that if a person has not been able to master his first dangers he is bound to come to grief as well in later situations involving sexual danger and thus be driven into a neurosis.

I do not believe, therefore, that Rank's attempt has solved the problem of the causation of neurosis; nor do I believe that we can say as yet how much it may nevertheless have *contributed* to such a solution. If an investigation into the effects of difficult birth on the disposition to neurosis should yield negative results, we shall rate the value of his contribution low. It is to be feared that our need to find a single, tangible 'ultimate cause' of neurotic illness will remain unsatisfied. The ideal solution, which medical men no doubt still yearn for, would be to discover some bacillus which could be isolated and bred in a pure culture and which, when injected into anyone, would invariably produce the same illness; or, to put it rather less extravagantly, to demonstrate the existence of certain chemical substances the administration of which would bring about or cure particular neuroses. But the probability of a solution of this kind seems slight.

Psycho-analysis leads to less simple and satisfactory conclusions. What I have to say in this connection has long been familiar and I have nothing new to add. If the ego succeeds in protecting itself from a dangerous instinctual impulse, through, for instance, the process of repression, it has certainly inhibited and damaged the particular part of the id concerned; but it has at the same time given it some independence and has renounced some of its own sovereignty. This is inevitable from the nature of repression, which is, fundamentally, an attempt at flight. The repressed is now, as it were, an outlaw; it is excluded from the great organization of the ego and is subject only to the laws which govern the realm of the unconscious. If, now, the danger-situation changes so that the ego has no reason for fending off a new instinctual impulse analogous to the repressed one, the consequence of the restriction of the ego which has taken place will become manifest. The new impulse will run its course under an automatic influence—or, as I should prefer to say, under the influence of the compulsion to repeat. It will follow the same path as the earlier, repressed impulse, as though the danger-situation that had been overcome still existed. The fixating factor in repression, then, is the unconscious id's compulsion to repeat—a compulsion which in normal circumstances is only done away with by the freely mobile function of the ego. The ego may occasionally manage to break down the barriers of repression which it has itself put up and to recover its influence over the instinctual impulse and direct the course of the new impulse in accordance with the changed danger-situation. But in point of fact the ego very seldom succeeds in doing this: it cannot undo its repressions. It is possible that the way the struggle will go depends upon quantitative relations. In some cases one has the impression that the outcome is an enforced one: the regressive attraction exerted by the repressed impulse and the strength of the repression are so great that the new impulse has no choice but to obey the compulsion to repeat. In other cases we perceive a contribution from another play of forces: the attraction exerted by the repressed prototype is reinforced by a repulsion coming from the direction of difficulties in real life which stand in the way of any different course that might be taken by the new instinctual impulse.

That this is a correct account of fixation upon repression and of the retention of danger-situations that are no longer present-day ones is confirmed by the fact of analytic therapy—a fact which is modest enough in itself but which can hardly be overrated from a theoretical point of view. When, in analysis, we have given the ego assistance which is able to put it in a position to lift its repressions, it recovers its power over the repressed id and can allow the instinctual impulses to run their course as though the old situations of danger no longer existed. What we can do in this way tallies with what can be achieved in other fields of medicine; for as a rule our therapy must be content with bringing about more quickly, more reliably and with less expenditure of energy than would otherwise be the case the good result which in favourable circumstances would have occurred of itself.

We see from what has been said that *quantitative* relations—relations which are not directly observable but which can only be inferred—are what determine whether or not old situations of danger shall be preserved, repressions on the part of the ego maintained and childhood neuroses find a continuation. Among the factors that play a part in the causation of neuroses and that have created the conditions under which the forces of the mind are pitted against one another, three emerge into prominence: a biological, a phylogenetic and a purely psychological factor.

The biological factor is the long period of time during which the young of the human species is in a condition of helplessness and dependence. Its intra-uterine existence seems to be short in comparison with that of most animals, and it is sent into the world in a less finished state. As a result, the influence of the real external world upon it is intensified and an early differentiation between the ego and the id is promoted. Moreover, the dangers of the external world have a greater importance for it, so that the value of the object which can alone protect it against them and take the place of its former intra-uterine life is enormously enhanced. The biological factor, then, establishes the earliest situations of danger and creates the need to be loved which will accompany the child through the rest of its life.

The existence of the second, phylogenetic, factor, is based only upon inference. We have been led to assume its existence by a remarkable feature in the development of the libido. We have found that the sexual life of man, unlike that of most of the animals nearly related to him, does not make a steady advance from birth to maturity, but that, after an early efflorescence up till the fifth year, it undergoes a very decided interruption; and that it then starts on its course once more at puberty, taking up again the beginnings broken off in early childhood. This has led us to suppose that something momentous must have occurred in the vicissitudes of the human species[3] which has left behind this

---

[3] [In Chapter III of *The Ego and the Id* (1923*b*), Freud makes it clear that he has the geological glacial epoch in mind. The idea had been put forward earlier by Ferenczi (1913).]

interruption in the sexual development of the individual as a historical precipitate. This factor owes its pathogenic significance to the fact that the majority of the instinctual demands of this infantile sexuality are treated by the ego as dangers and fended off as such, so that the later sexual impulses of puberty, which in the natural course of things would be ego-syntonic, run the risk of succumbing to the attraction of their infantile prototypes and following them into repression. It is here that we come upon the most direct aetiology of the neuroses. It is a curious thing that early contact with the demands of sexuality should have a similar effect on the ego to that produced by premature contact with the external world.

The third, psychological, factor resides in a defect of our mental apparatus which has to do precisely with its differentiation into an id and an ego, and which is therefore also attributable ultimately to the influence of the external world. In view of the dangers of [external] reality, the ego is obliged to guard against certain instinctual impulses in the id and to treat them as dangers. But it cannot protect itself from internal instinctual dangers as effectively as it can from some piece of reality that is not part of itself. Intimately bound up with the id as it is, it can only fend off an instinctual danger by restricting its own organization and by acquiescing in the formation of symptoms in exchange for having impaired the instinct. If the rejected instinct renews its attack, the ego is overtaken by all those difficulties which are known to us as neurotic ailments.

Further than this, I believe, our knowledge of the nature and causes of neurosis has not as yet been able to go.

XI
ADDENDA

In the course of this discussion various themes have had to be put aside before they had been fully dealt with. I have brought them together in this chapter so that they may receive the attention they deserve.

A. *Modifications of Earlier Views*

(A) RESISTANCE AND ANTICATHEXIS

An important element in the theory of repression is the view that repression is not an event that occurs once but that it requires a permanent expenditure [of energy]. If this expenditure were to cease, the repressed impulse, which is being fed all the time from its sources, would on the next occasion flow along the channels from which it had been forced away, and the repression would either fail in its purpose or would have to be repeated an indefinite number of times.[1] Thus it is because instincts are continuous in their nature that the ego has to make its defensive action secure by a permanent expenditure [of energy]. This action under-

---

[1] [Cf. the paper on 'Repression' (1915*d*), *Standard Ed.*, **14**, 151.]

taken to protect repression is observable in analytic treatment as *resistance*. Resistance presupposes the existence of what I have called *anticathexis*. An anticathexis of this kind is clearly seen in obsessional neurosis. It appears there in the form of an alteration of the ego, as a reaction-formation in the ego, and is effected by the reinforcement of the attitude which is the opposite of the instinctual trend that has to be repressed—as, for instance, in pity, conscientiousness and cleanliness. These reaction-formations of obsessional neurosis are essentially exaggerations of the normal traits of character which develop during the latency period. The presence of an anticathexis in hysteria is much more difficult to detect, though theoretically it is equally indispensable. In hysteria, too, a certain amount of alteration of the ego through reaction-formation is unmistakable and in some circumstances becomes so marked that it forces itself on our attention as the principal symptom. The conflict due to ambivalence, for instance, is resolved in hysteria by this means. The subject's hatred of a person whom he loves is kept down by an exaggerated amount of tenderness for him and apprehensiveness about him. But the difference between reaction-formations in obsessional neurosis and in hysteria is that in the latter they do not have the universality of a character-trait but are confined to particular relationships. A hysterical woman, for instance, may be specially affectionate with her own children whom at bottom she hates; but she will not on that account be more loving in general than other women or even more affectionate to other children. The reaction-formation of hysteria clings tenaciously to a particular object and never spreads over into a general disposition of the ego, whereas what is characteristic of obsessional neurosis is precisely a spreading-over of this kind—a loosening of relations to the object and a facilitation of displacement in the choice of object.

There is another kind of anticathexis, however, which seems more suited to the peculiar character of hysteria. A repressed instinctual impulse can be activated (newly cathected) from two directions: from within, through reinforcement from its internal sources of excitation, and from without, through the perception of an object that it desires. The hysterical anticathexis is mainly directed outwards, against dangerous perceptions. It takes the form of a special kind of vigilance which, by means of restrictions of the ego, causes situations to be avoided that would entail such perceptions, or, if they do occur, manages to withdraw the subject's attention from them. Some French analysts, in particular Laforgue [1926], have recently given this action of hysteria the special name of 'scotomization'.[2] This technique of anticathexis is still more noticeable in the phobias, whose interest is concentrated on removing the subject ever further from the possibility of the occurrence of the feared perception. The fact that anticathexis has an opposite direction in hysteria and the phobias from what it has in obsessional neurosis—though the distinction is not an absolute one— seems to be significant. It suggests that there is an intimate connection between repression and external anticathexis on the one hand and between regression and internal anticathexis (i.e. alteration in the ego through reaction-formation) on the other. The task of defence against a dangerous perception is, incidentally, common to all neuroses. Various commands and prohibitions in obsessional neurosis have the same end in view.

We showed on an earlier occasion[3] that the resistance that has to be overcome in analysis proceeds from the ego,

---

[2][Freud discussed this term at some length in his later paper on 'Fetishism' (1927e) in connection with the concept of disavowal (Verleugnung).]
[3][Towards the end of Chapter I of The Ego and the Id (1923b).]

which clings to its anticathexes. It is hard for the ego to direct its attention to perceptions and ideas which it has up till now made a rule of avoiding, or to acknowledge as belonging to itself impulses that are the complete opposite of those which it knows as its own. Our fight against resistance in analysis is based upon this view of the facts. If the resistance is itself unconscious, as so often happens owing to its connection with the repressed material, we make it conscious. If it is conscious, or when it has become conscious, we bring forward logical arguments against it; we promise the ego rewards and advantages if it will give up its resistance. There can be no doubt or mistake about the existence of this resistance on the part of the ego. But we have to ask ourselves whether it covers the whole state of affairs in analysis. For we find that even after the ego has decided to relinquish its resistances it still has difficulty in undoing the repressions; and we have called the period of strenuous effort which follows after its praiseworthy decision, the phase of 'working-through'.[4] The dynamic factor which makes a working-through of this kind necessary and comprehensible is not far to seek. It must be that after the ego's resistance has been removed the power of the compulsion to repeat— the attraction exerted by the unconscious prototype upon the repressed instinctual process—has still to be overcome. There is nothing to be said against describing this factor as the *resistance of the unconscious*. There is no need to be discouraged by these emendations. They are to be welcomed if they add something to our knowledge, and they are no disgrace to us so long as they enrich rather than invalidate our earlier views—by limiting some statement, perhaps, that

---

[4] [See 'Remembering, Repeating and Working-Through' (1914g) *Standard Ed.*, 12, 155–6. Freud returned to the subject in Section VI of his late technical paper 'Analysis Terminable and Interminable, (1937c).]

was too general or by enlarging some idea that was too narrowly formulated.

It must not be supposed that these emendations provide us with a complete survey of all the kinds of resistance that are met with in analysis. Further investigation of the subject shows that the analyst has to combat no less than five kinds of resistance, emanating from three directions—the ego, the id and the super-ego. The ego is the source of three of these, each differing in its dynamic nature. The first of these three ego-resistances is the *repression* resistance, which we have already discussed above [p. 91 ff.] and about which there is least new to be added. Next there is the *transference* resistance, which is of the same nature but which has different and much clearer effects in analysis, since it succeeds in establishing a relation to the analytic situation or the analyst himself and thus re-animating a repression which should only have been recollected.[5] The third resistance, though also an ego-resistance, is of quite a different nature. It proceeds from the *gain from illness* and is based upon an assimilation of the symptom into the ego. [See above, pp. 19–20 f.] It represents an unwillingness to renounce any satisfaction or relief that has been obtained. The fourth variety, arising from the *id,* is the resistance which, as we have just seen, necessitates 'working-through'. The fifth, coming from the *super-ego* and the last to be discovered, is also the most obscure though not always the least powerful one. It seems to originate from the sense of guilt or the need for punishment; and it opposes every move towards success, including, therefore, the patient's own recovery through analysis.[6]

---

[5][Cf. 'Remembering, Repeating and Working-Through' (1914*g*), *Standard Ed.,* 12, 151 ff.]
[6][This was discussed in the earlier part of Chapter V of *The Ego and the Id.*]

(B) ANXIETY FROM TRANSFORMATION OF LIBIDO

The view of anxiety which I have put forward in these pages diverges somewhat from the one I have hitherto thought correct. Formerly I regarded anxiety as a general reaction of the ego under conditions of unpleasure. I always sought to justify its appearance on economic grounds[7] and I assumed, on the strength of my investigations into the 'actual' neuroses, that libido (sexual excitation) which was rejected or not utilized by the ego found direct discharge in the form of anxiety. It cannot be denied that these various assertions did not go very well together, or at any rate did not necessarily follow from one another. Moreover, they gave the impression of there being a specially intimate connection between anxiety and libido and this did not accord with the general character of anxiety as a reaction to unpleasure.

The objection to this view arose from our coming to regard the ego as the sole seat of anxiety. It was one of the results of the attempt at a structural division of the mental apparatus which I made in *The Ego and the Id*. Whereas the old view made it natural to suppose that anxiety arose from the libido belonging to the repressed instinctual impulses, the new one, on the contrary, made the ego the source of anxiety. Thus it is a question of instinctual (id-) anxiety or ego-anxiety. Since the energy which the ego employs is desexualized, the new view also tended to weaken the close connection between anxiety and libido. I hope I have at least succeeded in making the contradiction plain and in giving a clear idea of the point in doubt.

Rank's contention—which was originally my own[8], that

---

[7]['*Ökonomisch.*' This word appears only in the first (1926) edition. It was omitted, no doubt by accident, in all the later ones.]
[8][See Editor's Introduction, p. xxxiv ff.]

the affect of anxiety is a consequence of the event of birth and a repetition of the situation then experienced, obliged me to review the problem of anxiety once more. But I could make no headway with his idea that birth is a trauma, states of anxiety a reaction of discharge to it and all subsequent affects of anxiety an attempt to 'abreact' it more and more completely. I was obliged to go back from the anxiety reaction to the *situation of danger* that lay behind it. The introduction of this element opened up new aspects of the question. Birth was seen to be the prototype of all later situations of danger which overtook the individual under the new conditions arising from a changed mode of life and a growing mental development. On the other hand its own significance was reduced to this prototypic relationship to danger. The anxiety felt at birth became the prototype of an affective state which had to undergo the same vicissitudes as the other affects. Either the state of anxiety reproduced itself *automatically* in situations analogous to the original situation and was thus an inexpedient form of reaction instead of an expedient one as it had been in the first situation of danger; or the ego acquired power over this affect, reproduced it on its own initiative, and employed it as a warning of danger and as a means of setting the pleasure-unpleasure mechanism in motion. We thus gave the biological aspect of the anxiety affect its due importance by recognizing anxiety as the general reaction to situations of danger; while we endorsed the part played by the ego as the seat of anxiety by allocating to it the function of producing the anxiety affect according to its needs. Thus we attributed two modes of origin to anxiety in later life. One was involuntary, automatic and always justified on economic grounds, and arose whenever a danger-situation analogous to birth had established itself. The other was produced by the ego as soon as a situation of this kind merely threatened to occur, in order to call for its avoidance. In the second case the ego subjects itself to anxiety as a sort of inoculation, submitting to a slight attack of the illness in order to escape its full strength. It vividly imagines the danger-situation, as it were, with the unmistakable purpose of restricting that distressing experience to a mere indication, a signal. We have already seen in detail [pp. 66–69] how the various situations of danger arise one after the other, retaining at the same time a genetic connection.

We shall perhaps be able to proceed a little further in our understanding of anxiety when we turn to the problem of the relation between neurotic anxiety and realistic anxiety [p. 101 ff.].

Our former hypothesis of a direct transformation of libido into anxiety possesses less interest for us now than it did. But if we do nevertheless consider it, we shall have to distinguish different cases. As regards anxiety evoked by the ego as a signal, it does not come into consideration; nor does it, therefore, in any of those danger-situations which move the ego to bring on repression. The libidinal cathexis of the repressed instinctual impulse is employed otherwise than in being transformed into anxiety and discharged as such—as is most clearly seen in conversion hysteria. On the other hand, further enquiry into the question of the danger-situation will bring to our notice an instance of the production of anxiety which will, I think, have to be accounted for in a different way [pp. 104–05].

(C) REPRESSION AND DEFENCE

In the course of discussing the problem of anxiety I have revived a concept or, to put it more modestly, a term, of which I made exclusive use thirty years ago when I first began to study the subject but which I later abandoned. I refer to the term 'defensive process'.[9] I afterwards replaced it by the word 'repression', but the relation between the two remained uncertain. It will be an undoubted advantage, I think, to revert to the old concept of 'defence', provided we employ it explicitly as a general designation for all the techniques which the ego makes use of in conflicts which may lead to a neurosis, while we retain the word 'repression' for the special method of defence which the line of approach taken by our investigations made us better acquainted with in the first instance.

Even a purely terminological innovation ought to justify its adoption; it ought to reflect some new point of view or some extension of knowledge. The revival of the concept of defence and the restriction of that of repression takes into account a fact which has long since been known but which has received added importance owing to some new discoveries. Our first observations of repression and of the formation of symptoms were made in connection with hysteria. We found that the perceptual content of exciting experiences and the ideational content of pathogenic structures of thought were forgotten and debarred from being reproduced in memory, and we therefore concluded that the keeping away from consciousness was a main characteristic of hysterical repression. Later on, when we came to study the obsessional neuroses, we found that in that illness pathogenic occurrences are not forgotten. They remain conscious but they are 'isolated' in some way that we cannot as yet grasp, so that much the same result is obtained as in hysterical amnesia. Nevertheless the difference is great enough to justify the belief that the process by which instinctual demands are set aside in obsessional neurosis cannot be the

---

[9]Cf. 'The Neuro-Psychoses of Defence' (1894a). [See Appendix A, p. 111 f.]

same as in hysteria. Further investigations have shown that in obsessional neurosis a regression of the instinctual impulses to an earlier libidinal stage is brought about through the opposition of the ego, and that this regression, although it does not make repression unnecessary, clearly works in the same sense as repression. We have seen, too, that in obsessional neurosis anticathexis, which is also presumably present in hysteria, plays a specially large part in protecting the ego by effecting a reactive alteration in it. Our attention has, moreover, been drawn to a process of 'isolation' (whose technique cannot as yet be elucidated) which finds direct symptomatic manifestation, and to a procedure, that may be called magical, of 'undoing' what has been done—a procedure about whose defensive purpose there can be no doubt, but which has no longer any resemblance to the process of 'repression'. These observations provide good enough grounds for re-introducing the old concept of *defence*, which can cover all these processes that have the same purpose—namely, the protection of the ego against instinctual demands—and for subsuming repression under it as a special case. The importance of this nomenclature is heightened if we consider the possibility that further investigations may show that there is an intimate connection between special forms of defence and particular illnesses, as, for instance, between repression and hysteria. In addition we may look forward to the possible discovery of yet another important correlation. It may well be that before its sharp cleavage into an ego and an id, and before the formation of a superego, the mental apparatus makes use of different methods of defence from those which it employs after it has reached these stages of organization.

B. Supplementary Remarks on Anxiety

The affect of anxiety exhibits one or two features the study of which promises to throw further light on the subject. Anxiety [*Angst*] has an unmistakable relation to *expectation:* it is anxiety *about* [10] something. It has a quality of *indefiniteness and lack of object.* In precise speech we use the word 'fear' [*Furcht*] rather than 'anxiety' [*Angst*] if it has found an object. Moreover, in addition to its relation to danger, anxiety has a relation to neurosis which we have long been trying to elucidate. The question arises: why are not all reactions of anxiety neurotic—why do we accept so many of them as normal? And finally the problem of the difference between realistic anxiety and neurotic anxiety awaits a thorough examination.

To begin with the last problem. The advance we have made is that we have gone behind reactions of anxiety to situations of danger. If we do the same thing with realistic anxiety we shall have no difficulty in solving the question. Real danger is a danger that is known, and realistic anxiety is anxiety about a known danger of this sort. Neurotic anxiety is anxiety about an unknown danger. Neurotic danger is thus a danger that has still to be discovered. Analysis has

---

[10][In German '*vor*,' literally 'before'. See similar discussions at the beginning of Chapter II of *Beyond the Pleasure Principle* (1920g), *Standard Ed.*, 18, 12 f., and in Lecture XXV of the *Introductory Lectures* (1916–17). It has not been possible in translation to render the German '*Angst*' invariably by 'anxiety'. In this volume, and throughout the *Standard Edition*, the word has sometimes been translated by 'fear' or by phrases including the word 'afraid', where English usage required it and confusion seemed unlikely. Some remarks on this will be found in the General Introduction in Volume I.]

shown that it is an instinctual danger. By bringing this danger which is not known to the ego into consciousness, the analyst makes neurotic anxiety no different from realistic anxiety, so that it can be dealt with in the same way.

There are two reactions to real danger. One is an affective reaction, an outbreak of anxiety. The other is a protective action. The same will presumably be true of instinctual danger. We know how the two reactions can co-operate in an expedient way, the one giving the signal for the other to appear. But we also know that they can behave in an inexpedient way: paralysis from anxiety may set in, and the one reaction spread at the cost of the other.

In some cases the characteristics of realistic anxiety and neurotic anxiety are mingled. The danger is known and real but the anxiety in regard to it is over-great, greater than seems proper to us. It is this surplus of anxiety which betrays the presence of a neurotic element. Such cases, however, introduce no new principle; for analysis shows that to the known real danger an unknown instinctual one is attached.

We can find out still more about this if, not content with tracing anxiety back to danger, we go on to enquire what the essence and meaning of a danger-situation is. Clearly, it consists in the subject's estimation of his own strength compared to the magnitude of the danger and in his admission of helplessness in the face of it—physical helplessness if the danger is real and psychical helplessness if it is instinctual. In doing this he will be guided by the actual experiences he has had. (Whether he is wrong in his estimation or not is immaterial for the outcome.) Let us call a situation of helplessness of this kind that has been actually experienced a *traumatic situation*. We shall then have good grounds for distinguishing a traumatic situation from a danger-situation.

The individual will have made an important advance in

his capacity for self-preservation if he can foresee and expect a traumatic situation of this kind which entails helplessness, instead of simply waiting for it to happen. Let us call a situation which contains the determinant for such an expectation a danger-situation. It is in this situation that the signal of anxiety is given. The signal announces: 'I am expecting a situation of helplessness to set in', or: 'The present situation reminds me of one of the traumatic experiences I have had before. Therefore I will anticipate the trauma and behave as though it had already come, while there is yet time to turn it aside.' Anxiety is therefore on the one hand an expectation of a trauma, and on the other a repetition of it in a mitigated form. Thus the two features of anxiety which we have noted have a different origin. Its connection with expectation belongs to the danger-situation, whereas its indefiniteness and lack of object belong to the traumatic situation of helplessness—the situation which is anticipated in the danger-situation.

Taking this sequence, anxiety—danger—helplessness (trauma), we can now summarize what has been said. A danger-situation is a recognized, remembered, expected situation of helplessness. Anxiety is the original reaction to helplessness in the trauma and is reproduced later on in the danger-situation as a signal for help. The ego, which experienced the trauma passively, now repeats it actively in a weakened version, in the hope of being able itself to direct its course. It is certain that children behave in this fashion towards every distressing impression they receive, by reproducing it in their play. In thus changing from passivity to activity they attempt to master their experiences psychically.[11] If this is what is meant by 'abreacting a trauma' we can no longer have anything to urge against the phrase. [See

---

[11][Cf. *Beyond the Pleasure Principle*, (1920g), *Standard Ed.*, 18, 16–17.]

p. 85.] But what is of decisive importance is the first displacement of the anxiety-reaction from its origin in the situation of helplessness to an expectation of that situation—that is, to the danger-situation. After that come the later displacements, from the danger to the determinant of the danger—loss of the object and the modifications of that loss with which we are already acquainted.

The undesirable result of 'spoiling' a small child is to magnify the importance of the danger of losing the object (the object being a protection against every situation of helplessness) in comparison with every other danger. It therefore encourages the individual to remain in the state of childhood, the period of life which is characterized by motor and psychical helplessness.

So far we have had no occasion to regard realistic anxiety in any different light from neurotic anxiety. We know what the distinction is. A real danger is a danger which threatens a person from an external object, and a neurotic danger is one which threatens him from an instinctual demand. In so far as the instinctual demand is something real, his neurotic anxiety, too, can be admitted to have a realistic basis. We have seen that the reason why there seems to be a specially close connection between anxiety and neurosis is that the ego defends itself against an instinctual danger with the help of the anxiety reaction just as it does against an external real danger, but that this line of defensive activity eventuates in a neurosis owing to an imperfection of the mental apparatus. We have also come to the conclusion that an instinctual demand often only becomes an (internal) danger because its satisfaction would bring on an external danger—that is, because the internal danger represents an external one.

On the other hand, the external (real) danger must also have managed to become internalized if it is to be significant for the ego. It must have been recognized as related to some situation of helplessness that has been experienced.[12] Man seems not to have been endowed, or to have been endowed to only a very small degree, with an instinctive recognition of the dangers that threaten him from without. Small children are constantly doing things which endanger their lives, and that is precisely why they cannot afford to be without a protecting object. In relation to the traumatic situation, in which the subject is helpless, external and internal dangers, real dangers and instinctual demands converge. Whether the ego is suffering from a pain which will not stop or experiencing an accumulation of instinctual needs which cannot obtain satisfaction, the economic situation is the same, and the motor helplessness of the ego finds expression in psychical helplessness.

In this connection the puzzling phobias of early childhood deserve to be mentioned once again. [Cf. p. 66.] We have been able to explain some of them, such as the fear of being alone or in the dark or with strangers, as reactions to the danger of losing the object. Others, like the fear of small animals, thunderstorms, etc., might perhaps be accounted for as vestigial traces of the congenital preparedness to meet real dangers which is so strongly developed in other animals. In man, only that part of this archaic heritage is appropriate which has reference to the loss of the object. If childhood phobias become fixated and grow stronger and persist into later years, analysis shows that their content has become

---

[12]It may quite often happen that although a danger-situation is correctly estimated in itself, a certain amount of instinctual anxiety is added to the realistic anxiety. In that case the instinctual demand before whose satisfaction the ego recoils is a masochistic one: the instinct of destruction directed against the subject himself. Perhaps an addition of this kind explains cases in which reactions of anxiety are exaggerated, inexpedient or paralysing. Phobias of heights (windows, towers, precipices and so on) may have some such origin. Their hidden feminine significance is closely connected with masochism. [Cf. 'Dreams and Telepathy' (1922*a*), *Standard Ed.*, 18, 213.]

associated with instinctual demands and has come to stand for internal dangers as well.

C. Anxiety, Pain and Mourning

So little is known about the psychology of emotional processes that the tentative remarks I am about to make on the subject may claim a very lenient judgement. The problem before us arises out of the conclusion we have reached that anxiety comes to be a reaction to the danger of a loss of an object. Now we already know one reaction to the loss of an object, and that is mourning. The question therefore is, when does that loss lead to anxiety and when to mourning? In discussing the subject of mourning on a previous occasion I found that there was one feature about it which remained quite unexplained. This was its peculiar painfulness. [Cf. p. 159–60.][13] And yet it seems self-evident that separation from an object should be painful. Thus the problem becomes more complicated: when does separation from an object produce anxiety, when does it produce mourning and when does it produce, it may be, only pain?

Let me say at once that there is no prospect in sight of answering these questions. We must content ourselves with drawing certain distinctions and adumbrating certain possibilities.

Our starting-point will again be the one situation which we believe we understand—the situation of the infant when it is presented with a stranger instead of its mother. It will exhibit the anxiety which we have attributed to the danger of loss of object. But its anxiety is undoubtedly more complicated than this and merits a more thorough discussion. That

---

[13]'Mourning and Melancholia' (1917e) [*Standard Ed.*, 14, 244–5].

it does have anxiety there can be no doubt; but the expression of its face and its reaction of crying indicate that it is feeling pain as well. Certain things seem to be joined together in it which will later on be separated out. It cannot as yet distinguish between temporary absence and permanent loss. As soon as it loses sight of its mother it behaves as if it were never going to see her again; and repeated consoling experiences to the contrary are necessary before it learns that her disappearance is usually followed by her reappearance. Its mother encourages this piece of knowledge which is so vital to it by playing the familiar game of hiding her face from it with her hands and then, to its joy, uncovering it again.[14] In these circumstances it can, as it were, feel longing unaccompanied by despair.

In consequence of the infant's misunderstanding of the facts, the situation of missing its mother is not a danger-situation but a traumatic one. Or, to put it more correctly, it is a traumatic situation if the infant happens at the time to be feeling a need which its mother should be the one to satisfy. It turns into a danger-situation if this need is not present at the moment. Thus, the first determinant of anxiety, which the ego itself introduces, is loss of perception of the object (which is equated with loss of the object itself). There is as yet no question of loss of love. Later on, experience teaches the child that the object can be present but angry with it; and then loss of love from the object becomes a new and much more enduring danger and determinant of anxiety.

The traumatic situation of missing the mother differs in one important respect from the traumatic situation of birth. At birth no object existed and so no object could be missed.

---

[14][Cf. the child's game described in Chapter II of *Beyond the Pleasure Principle, Standard Ed.*, 18, 14–16.]

Anxiety was the only reaction that occurred. Since then repeated situations of satisfaction have created an object out of the mother; and this object, whenever the infant feels a need, receives an intense cathexis which might be described as a 'longing' one. It is to this new aspect of things that the reaction of pain is referable. Pain is thus the actual reaction to loss of object, while anxiety is the reaction to the danger which that loss entails and, by a further displacement, a reaction to the danger of the loss of object itself.

We know very little about pain either. The only fact we are certain of is that pain occurs in the first instance and as a regular thing whenever a stimulus which impinges on the periphery breaks through the devices of the protective shield against stimuli and proceeds to act like a continuous instinctual stimulus, against which muscular action, which is as a rule effective because it withdraws the place that is being stimulated from the stimulus, is powerless.[15] If the pain proceeds not from a part of the skin but from an internal organ, the situation is still the same. All that has happened is that a portion of the inner periphery has taken the place of the outer periphery. The child obviously has occasion to undergo experiences of pain of this sort, which are independent of its experiences of need. This determinant of the generating of pain seems, however, to have very little similarity with the loss of an object. And besides, the element which is essential to pain, peripheral stimulation, is entirely absent in the child's situation of longing. Yet it cannot be for nothing that the common usage of speech should have created the notion of internal, mental pain and have treated the feeling of loss of object as equivalent to physical pain.

---

[15] [See *Beyond the Pleasure Principle*, ibid., 30–1, and the 'Project' (Freud, 1950*a*), Part I, Section 6.]

When there is physical pain, a high degree of what may be termed narcissistic cathexis of the painful place occurs.[16] This cathexis continues to increase and tends, as it were, to empty the ego.[17] It is well known that when internal organs are giving us pain we receive spatial and other presentations of parts of the body which are ordinarily not represented at all in conscious ideation. Again, the remarkable fact that, when there is a psychical diversion brought about by some other interest, even the most intense physical pains fail to arise (I must not say 'remain unconscious' in this case) can be accounted for by there being a concentration of cathexis on the psychical representative of the part of the body which is giving pain. I think it is here that we shall find the point of analogy which has made it possible to carry sensations of pain over to the mental sphere. For the intense cathexis of longing which is concentrated on the missed or lost object (a cathexis which steadily mounts up because it cannot be appeased) creates the same economic conditions as are created by the cathexis of pain which is concentrated on the injured part of the body. Thus the fact of the peripheral causation of physical pain can be left out of account. The transition from physical pain to mental pain corresponds to a change from narcissistic cathexis to object-cathexis. An object-presentation which is highly cathected by instinctual need plays the same role as a part of the body which is cathected by an increase of stimulus. The continuous nature of the cathectic process and the impossibility of inhibiting it produce the same state of mental helplessness. If the feeling of unpleasure which then arises has the specific character of pain (a character which cannot be more exactly

---

[16][Cf. 'On Narcissism' (1914c), *Standard Ed.*, **14**, 82.]
[17][See *Beyond the Pleasure Principle*, loc. cit., and an obscure passage in Section VI of Draft G (on melancholia) in the Fliess correspondence, probably dating from the beginning of January, 1895 (Freud, 1950a).]

described) instead of manifesting itself in the reactive form of anxiety, we may plausibly attribute this to a factor which we have not sufficiently made use of in our explanations— the high level of cathexis and 'binding' that prevails while these processes which lead to a feeling of unpleasure take place.[18]

We know of yet another emotional reaction to the loss of an object, and that is mourning. But we have no longer any difficulty in accounting for it. Mourning occurs under the influence of reality-testing; for the latter function demands categorically from the bereaved person that he should separate himself from the object, since it no longer exists.[19] Mourning is entrusted with the task of carrying out this retreat from the object in all those situations in which it was the recipient of a high degree of cathexis. That this separation should be painful fits in with what we have just said, in view of the high and unsatisfiable cathexis of longing which is concentrated on the object by the bereaved person during the reproduction of the situations in which he must undo the ties that bind him to it.

---

[18][See *Beyond the Pleasure Principle*, loc. cit., and the 'Project' (Freud 1950*a*), Part I, Section 12.]

[19]['Mourning and Melancholia' (1917*e*), *Standard Ed.*, 14, 244–5.]

APPENDIXES

A. 'Repression' and 'Defence'

The account which Freud gives on pp. 98–99 of the history of his use of the two terms is perhaps a little misleading, and in any case deserves amplification. Both of them occurred very freely during the Breuer period. The first appearance of 'repression *(Verdrängung)*' was in the 'Preliminary Communication' (1893*a*), *Standard Ed.*, **2**, 10, and of 'defence *(Abwehr)*'[1] in the first paper on 'The Neuro-Psychoses of Defence' (1894*a*). In the *Studies on Hysteria* (1895*d*), 'repression' appeared about a dozen times and 'defence' somewhat more often than that. There seems to have been some discrimination, however, between the use of the terms: 'repression' seems to have described the actual process, and 'defence' the motive for it. Nevertheless, in the preface to the first edition of the *Studies* (*Standard Ed.*, **2**, xxix) the authors appear to have equated the two concepts, for they spoke of their view that 'sexuality seems to play a principal part . . . as a motive for "defence"—that is, for repressing ideas from consciousness'. And, even more explicitly, Freud, in the first paragraph of his second paper on 'The Neuro-Psychoses of Defence' (1896*b*) alluded to the 'psychical process of "defence" or "repression" '.

---

[1] The corresponding verbal form used in the present edition is 'to fend off'.

After the Breuer period—that is, from about 1897 on-
wards—there was a falling-off in the frequency of the use of
'defence'. It was not dropped entirely, however, and will be
found several times, for instance, in Chapter VII of the first
edition of *The Psychopathology of Everyday Life* (1901*b*)
and in Section 7 of Chapter VII of the book on jokes
(1905*c*). But 'repression' was already beginning to predomi-
nate, and was almost exclusively used in the 'Dora' case
history (1905*e*) and the *Three Essays* (1905*d*). And soon
after this, attention was explicitly drawn to the change, in
a paper on sexuality in the neuroses (1906*a*), dated June,
1905. In the course of a survey of the historical development
of his views, and in dealing with the immediate post-Breuer
period, Freud had occasion to mention the concept and
wrote: '. . . "repression" (as I now began to say instead of
"defence") . . .' (*Standard Ed.*, 7, 276).

The slight inaccuracy which had begun to appear in this
sentence became more marked in a parallel phrase in the
'History of the Psycho-Analytic Movement' (1914*d*), *Standard Ed.*, 14, 11. Here Freud, once more writing of the end
of the Breuer period, remarked: 'I looked upon psychical
splitting itself as an effect of a process of repelling which at
that time I called "defence", and later, "repression".'

After 1905 the predominance of 'repression' increased
still more, till, for instance, in the 'Rat Man' analysis
(1909*d*), we find (*Standard Ed.*, 10, 196) Freud speaking of
'two kinds of repression', used respectively in hysteria and
obsessional neurosis. This is a specially plain example where,
on the revised scheme suggested in the present work, he
would have spoken of 'two kinds of *defence*'.

But it was not long before the usefulness of 'defence' as
a more inclusive term than 'repression' began unobtrusively
to make its appearance—particularly in the metapsychological papers. Thus, the 'vicissitudes' of the instincts, only one

of which is 'repression', were regarded as 'modes of *defence*' against them (*Standard Ed.*, 14, 127, 132 and 147), and, again, 'projection' was spoken of as a 'mechanism' or 'means of defence' (ibid., 184 and 224). Not until ten years later, however, in the present work, was the expediency of distinguishing between the use of the two terms explicitly recognized.

B. List of Writings by Freud Dealing Mainly or Largely with Anxiety

[*The topic of anxiety occurs in a very large number (perhaps in the majority) of Freud's writings. The following list may nevertheless be of some practical use. The date at the beginning of each entry is that of the year during which the work in question was probably written. The date at the end is that of publication, and under that date fuller particulars of the work will be found in the* Bibliography and Author Index. *The items in square brackets were published posthumously.*]

[1893   Draft B. 'The Aetiology of the Neuroses', Section II. (1950*a*)]

[1894   Draft E. 'How Anxiety Originates.' (1950*a*)]

[1894   Draft F. 'Collection III', No. 1. (1950*a*)]

[1895(?) Draft J. (1950*a*)]

1895   'Obsessions and Phobias', Section II. (1895*c*)

1895   'On the Grounds for Detaching a Particular Syndrome from Neurasthenia under the Description "Anxiety Neurosis".' (1895*b*)

1895   'A Reply to Criticisms of my Paper on Anxiety Neurosis.' (1895*f*)

1909   'Analysis of a Phobia in a Five-Year-Old Boy.'
        (1909*b*)

1910   ' "Wild" Psycho-Analysis.' (1910*k*)

1914   'From the History of an Infantile Neurosis.'
        (1918*b*)

1917   *Introductory Lectures on Psycho-Analysis*,
        Lecture XXV. (1916–17)

1925   *Inhibitions, Symptoms and Anxiety.* (1926*d*)

1932   *New Introductory Lectures on Psycho-Analysis*,
        Lecture XXXII (First Part). (1933*a*)

LIST OF ABBREVIATIONS

G.S.   = Freud, *Gesammelte Schriften* (12 vols.), Vienna, 1924–34

G.W.   = Freud, *Gesammelte Werke* (18 vols.), London, from 1940

C.P.   = Freud, *Collected Papers* (5 vols.), London, 1924–50

Standard Ed.   = Freud, *Standard Edition* (24 vols.), London from 1953

Almanach 1935 = *Almanach der Psychoanalyse 1935*, Vienna, Internationaler Psychoanalytischer Verlag, 1934

Almanach 1936 = *Almanach der Psychoanalyse 1936*, Vienna, Internationaler Psychoanalytischer Verlag, 1935

BIBLIOGRAPHY
AND AUTHOR INDEX

[Titles of books and periodicals are in italics; titles of papers are in inverted commas. Abbreviations are in accordance with the *World List of Scientific Periodicals* (London, 1952). Further abbreviations used in this volume will be found in the List at the end of the appendixes. Numerals in thick type refer to volumes; ordinary numerals refer to pages. The figures in round brackets at the end of each entry indicate the page or pages of this volume on which the work in question is mentioned. In the case of the Freud entries, the letters attached to the dates of publication are in accordance with the corresponding entries in the complete bibliography of Freud's writings to be included in the last volume of the *Standard Edition*.

For non-technical authors, and for technical authors where no specific work is mentioned, see the General Index.]

ADLER, A. (1907) *Studie über Minderwertigkeit von Organen,* Berlin and Vienna. (84)

[*Trans.: Study of Organ-Inferiority and its Psychical Compensation,* New York, 1917.]

BREUER, J., and FREUD, S. (1893) *See* FREUD, S. (1893*a*)

(1895) *See* FREUD, S. (1895*d*)

DARWIN, C. (1872) *The Expression of the Emotions in Man and Animals,* London. (xxxiv, 63)

FERENCZI, S. (1925) 'Zur Psychoanalyse von Sexualgewohnheiten', *Int. Z. Psychoan.,* 11, 6. (69)

[*Trans.:* 'Psycho-Analysis of Sexual Habits', *Further Contributions to the Theory and Technique of Psycho-Analysis,* London, 1926, Chap. XXXII.]

FREUD, S. (1893*a*) With BREUER, J., 'Über den psychischen Mechanismus hysterischer Phänomene: Vorläufige Mitteilung', *G.S.,* 1, 7; *G.W.,* 1, 81. (18, 111)

[*Trans.:* 'On the Psychical Mechanism of Hysterical Phenomena: Preliminary Communication', *C.P.*, 1, 24; *Standard Ed.*, 2, 3.]

(1894*a*) 'Die Abwehr-Neuropsychosen', *G.S.*, 1, 290; *G. W.*, 1, 59. (99, 111)

   [*Trans.:* 'The Neuro-Psychoses of Defence', *C.P.*, 1, 59; *Standard Ed.*, 3.]

(1895*b*) 'Über die Berechtigung, von der Neurasthenie einen bestimmten Symptomenkomplex als "Angstneurose" abzutrennen', *G.S.*, 1, 306; *G. W.*, 1, 315. (xxvii, xxix, xxxiv, 33, 62, 72, 111)

   [*Trans.:* 'On the Grounds for Detaching a Particular Syndrome from Neurasthenia under the Description "Anxiety Neurosis" ', *C.P.*, 1, 76; *Standard Ed.*, 3.]

(1895*c*) 'Obsessions et phobies' [in French], *G.S.*, 1, 334; *G. W.*, 1, 345. (114)

   [*Trans.:* 'Obsessions and Phobias', *C.P.*, 1, 128; *Standard Ed.*, 3.]

(1895*d*) With BREUER, J., *Studien über Hysterie*, Vienna. *G.S.*, 1, 3; *G. W.*, 1, 77 (omitting Breuer's contributions). (xxxiv, xxxiv, 18, 63, 111)

   [*Trans.: Studies on Hysteria*, *Standard Ed.*, 2, Including Breuer's contributions.]

(1895*f*) 'Zur Kritik der "Angstneurose" ', *G.S.*, 1, 343; *G. W.*, 1, 357. (115)

   [*Trans.:* 'A Reply to Criticisms of my Paper on Anxiety Neurosis', *C.P.*, 1, 107; *Standard Ed.*, 3.]

(1896*b*) 'Weitere Bemerkungen über die Abwehr-Neuropsychosen', *G.S.*, 1, 363; *G. W.*, 1, 379. (19, 38, 111)

   [*Trans.:* 'Further Remarks on the Neuro-Psychoses of Defence', *C.P.*, 1, 155; *Standard Ed.*, 3.]

(1900*a*) *Die Traumdeutung*, Vienna. *G.S.*, 2–3; *G. W.*, 2–3. (xxviii, xxxiii, xxxv, 55)

   [*Trans.: The Interpretation of Dreams*, London and New York, 1955; *Standard Ed.*, 4–5.]

(1901*b*) *Zur Psychopathologie des Alltagslebens*, Berlin, 1904. *G.S.*, 4, 3; *G. W.*, 4. (112)

   [*Trans.: The Psychopathology of Everyday Life*, *Standard Ed.*, 6.]

(1905*c*) *Der Witz und seine Beziehung zum Unbewussten*, Vienna. *G.S.*, 9, 5; *G. W.*, 6. (112)

   [*Trans.: Jokes and their Relation to the Unconscious*, *Standard Ed.*, 8.]

(1905*d*) *Drei Abhandlungen zur Sexualtheorie*, Vienna. *G.S.*, 5, 3; *G. W.*, 5, 29. (xxviii, xxxi, xxxiv, 9, 67, 112)

[*Trans.: Three Essays on the Theory of Sexuality*, London, 1949; *Standard Ed.*, 7, 125.]

(1905*e* [1901]) 'Bruchstück einer Hysterie-Analyse', *G.S.*, 8, 3; *G.W.*, 5, 163. (112)

[*Trans.:* 'Fragment of an Analysis of a Case of Hysteria', *C.P.*, 3, 13; *Standard Ed.*, 7, 3.]

(1906*a*) 'Meine Ansichten über die Rolle der Sexualität in der Ätiologie der Neurosen', *G.S.*, 5, 123; *G.W.*, 5, 149. (112)

[*Trans.:* 'My Views on the Part played by Sexuality in the Aetiology of the Neuroses', *C.P.*, 1, 272; *Standard Ed.*, 7, 271.]

(1907*a*) *Der Wahn und die Träume in W. Jensens 'Gradiva'*, Vienna, *G.S.*, 9, 273; *G.W.*, 7, 31. (xxviii)

[*Trans.: Delusions and Dreams in Jensen's 'Gradiva'*, *Standard Ed.*, 9, 3.]

(1908*f*) Preface to Stekel's *Nervöse Angstzustände und ihre Behandlung*, *G.S.*, 11, 239; *G.W.*, 7, 467. (xxxv)

[*Trans.: Standard Ed.*, 9, 250.]

(1909*a*) 'Allgemeines über den hysterischen Anfall', *G.S.*, 5, 255; *G.W.*, 7, 235. (xxxiv)

[*Trans.:* 'Some General Remarks on Hysterical Attacks', *C.P.*, 2, 100; *Standard Ed.*, 9, 229.]

(1909*b*) 'Analyse der Phobie eines fünfjährigen Knaben', *G.S.*, 8, 129; *G.W.*, 7, 243. (xxxi, xxxvi, 22–26, 28–31, 51–54, 58, 115)

[*Trans.:* 'Analysis of a Phobia in a Five-Year-Old Boy', *C.P.*, 3, 149; *Standard Ed.*, 10, 3.]

(1909*d*) 'Bemerkungen über einen Fall von Zwangsneurose', *G.S.*, 8, 269; *G.W.*, 7, 381. (43, 45, 47, 112)

[*Trans.:* 'Notes upon a Case of Obsessional Neurosis', *C.P.*, 3, 293; *Standard Ed.*, 10, 155.]

(1910*a* [1909]) *Über Psychoanalyse*, Vienna. *G.S.*, 4, 349; *G.W.*, 8, 3. (12, 55)

[*Trans.:* 'Five Lectures on Psycho-Analysis', *Amer. J. Psychol.*, 21 (1910), 181; *Standard Ed.*, 11, 3.]

(1910*h*) 'Über einen besonderen Typus der Objektwahl beim Manne', *G.S.*, 5, 186; *G.W.*, 8, 66. (xxxv–xxxvi)

[*Trans.:* 'A Special Type of Choice of Object made by Men', *C.P.*, 4, 192; *Standard Ed.*, 11, 165.]

(1910*k*) 'Über "wilde" Psychoanalyse', *G.S.*, 6, 37; *G.W.*, 8, 118. (115)

[*Trans.:* ' "Wild" Psycho-Analysis', *C.P.*, 2, 297; *Standard Ed.*, 11, 221.]

(1912–13) *Totem und Tabu*, Vienna, 1913. *G.S.*, 10, 3; *G.W.*, 9. (49)

[*Trans.: Totem and Taboo*, London, 1950; New York, 1952; *Standard Ed.*, **13**, 1.]

(1913*i*) 'Die Disposition zur Zwangsneurose', *G.S.*, **5**, 277; *G.W.*, **8**, 442. (39)

[*Trans.:* 'The Disposition to Obsessional Neurosis', *C.P.*, **2**, 122; *Standard Ed.*, **12**, 313.]

(1914*c*) 'Zur Einführung des Narzissmus', *G.S.*, **6**, 155; *G.W.*, **10**, 138. (109)

[*Trans.:* 'On Narcissism: an Introduction', *C.P.*, **4**, 30; *Standard Ed.*, **14**, 69.]

(1914*d*) 'Zur Geschichte der psychoanalytischen Bewegung', *G.S.*, **4**, 411; *G.W.*, **10**, 44. (112)

[*Trans.:* 'On the History of the Psycho-Analytic Movement', *C.P.*, **1**, 287; *Standard Ed.*, **14**, 3.]

(1914*g*) 'Weitere Ratschläge zur Technik der Psychoanalyse: II. Erinnern, Wiederholen und Durcharbeiten', *G.S.*, **6**, 109; *G.W.*, **10**, 126. (94, 95)

[*Trans.:* 'Recollecting, Repeating and Working-Through (Further Recommendations on the Technique of Psycho-Analysis, II)', *C.P.*, **2**, 366; *Standard Ed.*, **12**, 147.]

(1915*c*) 'Triebe und Triebschicksale', *G.S.*, **5**, 443; *G.W.*, **10**, 210, (11, 28, 113)

[*Trans.:* 'Instincts and their Vicissitudes', *C.P.*, **4**, 60; *Standard Ed.*, **14**, 111.]

(1915*d*) 'Die Verdrängung', *G.S.*, **5**, 466; *G.W.*, **10**, 248. (xxviii, xxix, 9, 32, 78, 91, 112)

[*Trans.:* 'Repression', *C.P.*, **4**, 84; *Standard Ed.*, **14**, 143.]

(1915*e*) 'Das Unbewusste', *G.S.*, **5**, 480; *G.W.*, **10**, 264. (xxix, xxxiii, 54, 71, 78, 112)

[*Trans.:* 'The Unconscious', *C.P.*, **4**, 98; *Standard Ed.*, **14**, 161.]

(1916–17) *Vorlesungen zur Einführung in die Psychoanalyse*, Vienna. *G.S.*, **7**; *G.W.*, **11**. (xxx, xxxiii, xxxiv, xxxv, 20, 37, 101, 115)

[*Trans.: Introductory Lectures on Psycho-Analysis*, revised ed., London, 1929 (*A General Introduction to Psychoanalysis*, New York, 1935); *Standard Ed.*, **15–16**.]

(1917*a*) 'Eine Schwierigkeit der Psychoanalyse', *G.S.*, **10**, 347; *G.W.*, **12**, 3. (25)

[*Trans.:* 'A Difficulty in the Path of Psycho-Analysis', *C.P.*, **4**, 347; *Standard Ed.*, **17**, 137.]

(1917*d* [1915]) 'Metapsychologische Ergänzung zur Traumlehre', *G.S.*, **5**, 520; *G.W.*, **10**, 412. (55)

[*Trans.:* 'A Metapsychological Supplement to the Theory of Dreams', *C.P.*, **4**, 137; *Standard Ed.*, **14**, 219.]

(1917*e* [1915]) 'Trauer und Melancholie', *G.S.*, **5**, 535; *G.W.*, **10**, 428. (59, 106, 110)

[*Trans.:* 'Mourning and Melancholia', *C.P.*, **4**, 152; *Standard Ed.*, **14**, 239.]

(1918*b* [1914]) 'Aus der Geschichte einer infantilen Neurose', *G.S.*, **8**, 439; *G.W.*, **12**, 29. (26–32, 38, 51–54, 70, 115)

[*Trans.:* 'From the History of an Infantile Neurosis', *C.P.*, **3**, 473; *Standard Ed.*, **17**, 3.]

(1919*d*) Einleitung zu *Zur Psychoanalyse der Kriegsneurosen*, Vienna. *G.S.*, **11**, 252; *G.W.*, **12**, 321. (58)

[*Trans.:* Introduction to *Psycho-Analysis and the War Neuroses*, London and New York, 1921. *C.P.*, **5**, 83; *Standard Ed.*, **17**, 207.]

(1920*g*) *Jenseits des Lustprinzips*, Veinna. *G.S.*, **6**, 191; *G.W.*, **13**, 3. (10, 13, 62, 101, 103, 107, 108, 109)

[*Trans.:* *Beyond the Pleasure Principle*, London, 1950; *Standard Ed.*, **18**, 3.]

(1922*a*) 'Traum und Telepathie', *G.S.*, **3**, 278; *G.W.*, **13**, 165. (105)

[*Trans.:* 'Dreams and Telepathy', *C.P.*, **4**, 408; *Standard Ed.*, **18**, 197.]

(1923*b*) *Das Ich und das Es*, Vienna. *G.S.*, **6**, 353; *G.W.*, **13**, 237. (xxxii, xxxvi–xxxvii, 15, 39, 58, 71, 89, 93, 95)

[*Trans.:* *The Ego and the Id*, London, 1927; *Standard Ed.*, **19**.]

(1924*d*) 'Der Untergang des Ödipuskomplexes', *G.S.*, **5**, 423; *G.W.*, **13**, 395. (xxxii, 74)

[*Trans.:* 'The Dissolution of the Oedipus Complex', *C.P.*, **2**, 269 *Standard Ed.*, **19**.]

(1925*j*) 'Einige psychische Folgen des anatomischen Geschlechtsunterschieds', *G.S.*, **11**, 8; *G.W.*, **14**, 19. (xxxi–xxxii, 75)

[*Trans.:* 'Some Psychical Consequences of the Anatomical Distinction between the Sexes', *C.P.*, **5**, 186; *Standard Ed.*, **19**.]

(1926*a*) 'An Romain Rolland', *G.S.*, **11**, 275; *G.W.*, **14**, 553.

[*Trans.:* 'To Romain Rolland', *Standard Ed.*, **20**, 279.]

(1926*b*) 'Karl Abraham', *G.S.*, **11**, 283; *G.W.*, **14**, 564.

[*Trans.:* 'Karl Abraham', *Int. J. Psycho-Anal.*, **7**, 1; *Standard Ed.*, **20**, 277.]

(1926*d*) *Hemmung, Symptom und Angst*, Vienna. *G.S.*, **11**, 23; *G.W.*, **14**, 113. (115)

[*Trans.:* *Inhibitions, Symptoms and Anxiety*, London, 1936 (The *Problem of Anxiety*, New York, 1936); *Standard Ed.*, **20**, 77.]

(1926f) An Article in the *Encyclopaedia Britannica* [published as 'Psycho-Analysis: Freudian School'], *Encyclopaedia Britannica*, 13th ed., New Vol. 3, 253; *Standard Ed.*, 20, 261.

[*German Text:* 'Psycho-Analysis', *G.S.*, 12, 372; *G.W.*, 14, 299. German original first appeared in 1934.]

(1927e) 'Fetischismus', *G.S.*, 11, 395; *G.W.*, 14, 311. (93)

[*Trans.:* 'Fetishism', *C.P.*, 5, 198; *Standard Ed.*, 21.]

(1930a) *Das Unbehagen in der Kultur*, Vienna. *G.S.*, 12, 29; *G.W.*, 14, 421. (57)

[*Trans.: Civilization and its Discontents*, London and New York, 1930; *Standard Ed.*, 21.]

(1933a) *Neue Folge der Vorlesungen zur Einführung in die Psychoanalyse*, Vienna. *G.S.*, 12, 151; *G.W.*, 15, 207. (xxix, xxx, 15, 101)

[*Trans.: New Introductory Lectures on Psycho-Analysis*, London and New York, 1933; *Standard Ed.*, 22.]

(1937c) 'Die endliche und die unendliche Analyse', *G.W.*, 16, 59. (94)

[*Trans.:* 'Analysis Terminable and Interminable', *C.P.*, 5, 316; *Standard Ed.*, 23.]

(1941e [1926]) Ansprache an die Mitglieder des Vereins *B'nai B'rith*, *G.W.*, 17, 51.

[*Trans.:* Address to the Members of the *B'nai B'rith*, *Standard Ed.*, 20, 273.]

(1950a [1887–1902]) *Aus den Anfängen der Psychoanalyse*, London. Includes 'Entwurf einer Psychologie' (1895). (xxvii, xxviii, xxxi, xxxiii, xxxiv, 10, 108, 109, 110)

[*Trans.: The Origins of Psycho-Analysis*, London and New York, 1954. (Partly, including 'A Project for a Scientific Psychology', in *Standard Ed.*, 1.)]

JONES, E. (1957) *Sigmund Freud: Life and Work*, Vol. 3, London and New York. (Page references are to the English edition.) (xxvi, xxvii, xxxvii)

LAFORGUE, R. (1926) 'Verdrängung und Skotomisation', *Int. Z. Psychoan.*, 12, 54. (93)

RANK, O. (1924) *Das Trauma der Geburt*, Vienna. (xxxvi–xxxvii, 65–66, 84–87, 96–97)

[*Trans.: The Trauma of Birth*, London, 1929.]

REIK, T. (1925) *Geständniszwang und Strafbedürfnis*, Leipzig, Vienna and Zurich. (43)

RIE, O. and FREUD, S. (1891) *See* FREUD, S. (1891a)

STEKEL, W. (1908) *Nervöse Angstzustände und ihre Behandlung*, Berlin and Vienna. (xxxvi)

GENERAL INDEX

This index includes the names of non-technical authors. It also includes the names of technical authors where no reference is made in the text to specific works. For references to specific technical works, the Bibliography should be consulted.—The compilation of the index was undertaken by Mrs. R. S. Partridge.